The Welfare State: A Very Short Introduction

VERY SHORT INTRODUCTIONS are for anyone wanting a stimulating and accessible way into a new subject. They are written by experts, and have been translated into more than 40 different languages.

The series began in 1995, and now covers a wide variety of topics in every discipline. The VSI library now contains over 450 volumes—a Very Short Introduction to everything from Psychology and Philosophy of Science to American History and Relativity—and continues to grow in every subject area.

Very Short Introductions available now:

For more information visit our website

www.oup.com/vsi/

David Garland

THE WELFARE STATE

A Very Short Introduction

OXFORD
UNIVERSITY PRESS

Great Clarendon Street, Oxford, OX2 6DP,
United Kingdom

Oxford University Press is a department of the University of Oxford.
It furthers the University's objective of excellence in research, scholarship,
and education by publishing worldwide. Oxford is a registered trade mark of
Oxford University Press in the UK and in certain other countries

Published in the United States of America by Oxford University Press
198 Madison Avenue, New York, NY 10016, United States of America

British Library Cataloguing in Publication Data
Data available

Library of Congress Control Number: 2015955583

ISBN 978-0-19-967266-0

Printed in Great Britain by
Ashford Colour Press Ltd, Gosport, Hampshire

Contents

Acknowledgements

I would like to thank the following colleagues, friends, and loved ones for their generous assistance and advice: Mike Adler, Michelle Austin, Vanessa Barker, Yvette Bisono, Craig Calhoun, Oscar Chase, Tom Daems, David Donnison, David Downes, Gretchen Feltes, Amy Garland, Bernard Harcourt, Anton Hemerdijk, Henner Hess, Stephen Holmes, Dan Hulsebosch, Jim Jacobs, David Kamin, Michael Meranze, Lindsay Paterson, Robert Reiner, Mike Rowan, Dan Shaviro, and Anna Skarpelis. I am also indebted to the New York University doctoral students who took my welfare state seminar and taught me a great deal in the process; to three anonymous referees who provided comments on my proposal; to New York University School of Law's Filomen D'Agostino and Max E. Greenberg Research Fund, and to Jenny Nugee and Andrea Keegan, my editors at Oxford University Press. This book is dedicated to my daughters, Amy and Kasia Garland, and to my wife, Anne Jowett, who makes everything possible.

List of illustrations

Chapter 1
What is the welfare state?

What, in fact, *is* the welfare state? If you are reading this book, the chances are good that you live in a society with a highly developed welfare state and that you have, at various points in your life, come to depend on welfare state institutions. It is also quite likely that you have definite views about the welfare state—whether for or against—and that these views inform your voting behaviour, your political identity, and your attitude towards government. Those of us who live in developed societies are involved with welfare state institutions in all sorts of ways on an almost daily basis: and conflicts over welfare state policies—and the taxes that fund them—are always at the forefront of political debate.

Yet despite these involvements, very few of us could give an accurate account of what the welfare state is, what its institutions do, and what effects they have—let alone discuss its history and the different forms it can take. Welfare states are familiar, even mundane, but their true character remains elusive. And more often than not our supposed understandings turn out to be misunderstandings based on myths and misrepresentations that pass themselves off as facts.

One way of misunderstanding the welfare state is to view it as a thing of the past. Political commentators often talk of the welfare state in the past tense as though it were a historic episode that is no longer with us: a post-war era of social solidarity—or 'big government'—long since killed off by market forces and neoliberal reforms. But the idea that welfare states have passed into history confuses ongoing processes of conflict and reform with much more fundamental processes of structural change. As we will see, welfare states are frequently under attack and their character has changed over time but the welfare state remains a fundamental dimension of modern government. Reports of its demise are altogether exaggerated.

Another way of misunderstanding the welfare state is to demonize it: to portray it as a 'narcotic that saps the spirit', a drag on growth and industry, or a totalitarian bureaucracy that crushes individual freedom. Such descriptions are a staple of political debate—as when American opponents of the welfare state portray it as 'socialism' and 'class war'; or when Tony Blair characterizes UK welfare expenditures as 'bills of social failure'. But as empirical claims they are, as we will see, very wide of the mark.

These negative depictions are related to another common misrepresentation: the tendency to reduce the welfare state's expansive range of social provision to a narrow notion of 'welfare for the poor'. This straitened conception identifies welfare states with their least popular and most problematic aspects ('handouts', 'doles', 'dependency', and so on) and depicts welfare recipients as unproductive scroungers. In reality, welfare states are much broader and more all-encompassing sets of institutions that insure and provide for most of the population, benefit the middle classes more than the poor, and can have a very positive impact on economic growth and prosperity. Nevertheless, false conceptions such as these are very influential—even among people who should know better (see Box 1).

What I want to do in this *Very Short Introduction* is to offer a more accurate and more illuminating characterization of the welfare state—one that builds on the research of historians, sociologists,

Box 1 Misrepresenting the welfare state

Interviewer: 'Is it a problem if the Labour Party is seen as the party of the welfare state?'

Ed Miliband: 'Yes, of course, but we're not. We don't want to be seen, and we're not, the party to represent those who are out of work...We are the Labour Party we are not the party of people on benefits.'

Labour Party leader, Ed Miliband, during a televised election debate, April 2015

and comparative social policy scholars to provide an accessible, realistic understanding. I will argue that the welfare state should be viewed not as a moment in post-war history, a radical left-wing politics, a questionable handout to the poor, or a drag on the economy but instead as a fundamental aspect of modern government—universally present in all advanced societies in one form or another—that operates as an indispensable means of making capitalist economies socially and economically sustainable. Among social scientists, the normality and functional necessity of welfare states in capitalist democracies is a settled empirical claim. That this social scientific view is not more widely shared is a consequence of the powerful political forces ranged against the welfare state and their distorting effects on public perception.

The 'welfare state' as misnomer

Some of our misunderstandings about the welfare state flow from the name it has been given. Welfare states are not primarily about 'welfare' and certainly not primarily about welfare for the poor. They are about social insurance, social rights, social provision, and the social regulation of economic action—the chief beneficiaries of which are not the poor but the middle classes and those in employment.

3

Nor is the welfare state necessarily about the state or state institutions. It is true that welfare state programmes are legislated and funded by government and depend, for the most part, on taxation and legal compulsion. But the services and benefits these programmes provide need not be produced, administered, or delivered by state officials. In Germany and several other European nations the administration of social insurance and the delivery of social services are entrusted to religious and voluntary associations. In Canada, healthcare is privately provided but medical providers are paid by a government insurance fund. And in the USA, a great deal of tax-funded welfare—in the form of high-cost health care and retirement pensions—is distributed in and through private corporations as compensation to well-paid employees.

Nor is 'the welfare state' an appropriate way to describe the state as a whole, as if the whole of government were taken up with the task of social provision. No modern state—not even post-war Britain or Sweden in the 1960s—'is' a welfare state. Properly used, the concept only ever refers to a specific mode of governing and a specific sector of governmental activity. The welfare state is one dimension of a much larger state that pursues other ends, carries out other functions, and incurs other forms of expenditure.

On the other hand, it is striking that there is no state in the industrialized world that *lacks* a developed welfare state apparatus that absorbs a significant fraction of public expenditure. Welfare state regimes take a great variety of forms, and some are more extensive or generous than others; but the existence of a welfare state is a feature of all developed societies. That is a significant social fact.

The welfare state's name has always been a problem. When the phrase first entered common usage in the 1950s and 1960s, it was least popular with the people most closely associated with the institutions it purported to describe. William Beveridge—the social reformer and administrator generally regarded as the father of the British welfare state—heartily disliked the term. He objected that it implied a 'something for nothing', 'Santa Claus state' quite at odds with his stress on the importance of worker contributions, voluntary effort, and personal responsibility. T. H. Marshall—the welfare state theorist who gave us our modern conceptions of social rights and social citizenship—also avoided the term. In his famous lecture on *Citizenship and Social Class* Marshall never once used the phrase and he later declared that 'the welfare state is a term for which I have developed a very strong dislike'. Even Richard Titmuss, the leading academic spokesman for Britain's post-war social policies, regarded 'the welfare state' as a hostile phrase, used by social policy's enemies rather than its friends.

What Beveridge, Marshall, and Titmuss understood is that the welfare state phrase tends to evoke images of a mendicant clientele receiving undeserved benefits from an overbearing state. That the name eventually became established, and used by supporter and opponent alike, has meant that these negative associations remain just beneath the surface and are all-too-easily brought to mind. If we could wave a wand and change the language, it would be more accurate (and less Anglo-centric) to talk of 'the social state' and 'welfare capitalism'. But after half a century of widespread usage we are probably stuck with the phrase so I will continue to use it here. But readers have been warned...

What is the welfare state?

Actual welfare states are as varied as the nations in which they exist. The expansive, egalitarian welfare state of social democratic Sweden stands in marked contrast to the more minimal, market-oriented version that exists in the USA. But Sweden's welfare state also differs in important ways from the welfare

states of other social democratic nations, including those of
its Nordic neighbours with whom it is usually grouped. And
America's welfare institutions are quite different from those of
Canada, Australia, or New Zealand, even though these nations
are usually categorized together as 'liberal' welfare regimes.
(The term 'liberal' is used in comparative social policy to mean
market-oriented. Confusingly, this is almost the opposite of
American political usage where 'liberal' has come to mean
supportive of activist government.) America's welfare state also
varies within itself, with the fifty states and innumerable city
governments establishing different policies and services for
their residents.

Welfare states also change over time. They evolve and undergo
reform, whether at the day-to-day level of administration or at the
more fundamental level of policies and objectives. Franklin D.
Roosevelt's New Deal established the American welfare state. But
FDR's welfare state was revised and extended by Johnson's Great
Society reforms and subsequently re-engineered by Clinton's
'welfare to work' legislation, just as the welfare state created in
Britain by post-war Labour government leaders such as Clement
Atlee and Nye Bevan has been extensively reworked and reformed
in the decades since.

So welfare states vary over time and cross-nationally. But beneath
this variation there is a shared foundation—a specific mode of
exercising government power and a specific set of conceptions,
institutions, and techniques with which to do so. And it is this
distinctive mode of welfare state government that I want to
describe and explain.

In my initial discussion, I will talk about the welfare state *in
general*, as a mode of government and an institutional dimension
of modern society, rather than about particular welfare state
policies, programmes, or practices. In this regard, my approach
is a little unusual. Because the web of welfare state practices is,

in every nation, a densely-woven one, involving a multitude of laws, programmes, and agencies—each with its own technical details, legislative history, and interest group politics—academic discussions are mostly about specific programmes rather than about the welfare state as a whole. But if we are to grasp the larger issues at stake—and appreciate the welfare state's overall functioning, the values it embodies, and the interests it represents—we need to consider the larger picture of which these programmes form a part. By viewing the welfare state as a distinctive phenomenon—a modern mode of government with its own distinctive characteristics—we can better understand its historic significance and the role it plays in contemporary societies.

Three welfare state conceptions

So what, exactly, is this welfare state to which I have been referring? Experts in this field generally utilize one of three rather different conceptions of the welfare state, each with a distinct set of boundaries and a distinctive account of the welfare state's functions.

The first of these characterizes the welfare state as welfare for the poor. This is the narrowest conception and the one preferred by the welfare state's opponents. It refers to the most problematic and least popular aspects of the system: namely the non-contributory, means-tested relief involved in American programmes such as Temporary Assistance to Needy Families (TANF), food stamps, and General Assistance or programmes such as Income Support or Job Seeker's Allowance (JSA) that exist in the UK. This is the conception invoked in American political discourse—and increasingly in Britain too—whenever 'welfare' or the 'welfare system' is being criticized.

A second approach focuses on social insurance, social rights, and social services. This is the analytical approach of most comparative social policy research and includes the institutions—Social Security and Medicare in the US; National Insurance and the National Health Service (NHS) in the UK—that account for most government social expenditure. It also includes public education: a form of social provision that predates the welfare state but which has become a fundamental social right in the welfare state context. (In the UK, about 20 per cent of government spending currently goes on pensions; 18 per cent on healthcare; 12 per cent on education; and 20 per cent on all other forms of welfare combined.) These core elements of the welfare state are abidingly popular with the electorate, and are supported even by avowedly anti-government political movements such as the Tea Party.

The third conception highlights economic management and the role that the government of the economy plays in every welfare state. This is the broadest delineation and the one least familiar in public debate but it is the conception used by political economists and sociologists and will be central to the analysis I develop here. This broader conception highlights the government's regulatory, fiscal, monetary, and labour-market policies and their role in shaping markets, promoting growth, providing employment, and ensuring the welfare of firms and families. And although this dimension is frequently overlooked in social policy textbooks—which tend to leave it to the economists—it is a fundamental and continuing feature of welfare state government.

These three conceptions are usually seen as competing characterizations of what the welfare state is. But rather than choose between them, we ought to view them as concentric circles of welfare state government, each one forming a structurally integrated element of the whole. At the core of the welfare state complex are the institutions—'mechanisms of security' as the philosopher Michel Foucault called them—that insure against loss of earnings by reason of unemployment, ill-health, old-age, disability, and so on. The operation of these insurance schemes, pitched at a national scale, affecting the whole population, and accounting for a significant fraction of GDP, is itself a mode of economic governance. These schemes, in turn, depend for their solvency on government policies that raise taxes, sustain employment, and promote growth, while simultaneously contributing to these ends by smoothing consumption, enhancing labour flexibility, providing economic stability, and enabling counter-cyclical spending. Social insurance schemes are, in turn, supplemented by a non-contributory 'safety net' for those individuals who are uninsured. No one of these three sectors can exist in that form without the others as structural supports: each is a condition of existence of the other.

If the capitalist economy is a dynamic machine for generating private profits by means of competitive production and market exchange, the welfare state is a retrofitted set of gears, brakes, and distributors, designed to steer the capitalist juggernaut along a more socially acceptable course. At its core is a set of social protections, superimposed upon capitalist economic processes, designed to modify and moralize the market economy. These protections take a variety of forms and may be financed by payroll contributions, general taxation, or government borrowing. They insure workers and their families against the hazards of injury, sickness, unemployment, and old age; provide individuals with social rights to education, housing, healthcare, and social services; and make a safety net of discretionary social assistance available in cases of unmet need.

The welfare state's pragmatism

Welfare states are varied, complex, and difficult to define. There is no simple theory that clearly expresses what they do; no simple vision that neatly captures what they are for. This complexity and variability also creates difficulties for the welfare state's advocates. Unlike its historic competitors—free-market capitalism on the one hand and state socialism on the other—the welfare state lacks utopian ideals and a pantheon of heroic proponents. It was a product not of revolutionary idealism but of piecemeal reform and cross-class coalitions. Its principles were created not by visionary philosophers but by civil servants, social scientists, and government committees that strove to forge compromises and work out practical arrangements. Arguments for the welfare state are more often phrased as technocratic recipes than as impassioned ideals—despite the efforts of thinkers such as John Rawls, Ronald Dworkin, Martha Nussbaum, and Amartya Sen and the powerful claims they have made on behalf of social justice, equality, solidarity, and the importance of developing capabilities to foster freedom.

As a result, welfare states rarely command unbridled enthusiasm. Being committed to compromise and 'middle way' solutions, they open themselves to attack from both Right and Left. Being ameliorative rather than curative, they rarely achieve complete success or large-scale victories. Being technocratic rather than ideological, welfare state experts have trouble connecting to a larger public and their preoccupation with evaluation and reform tends to highlight the system's shortcomings, allowing its virtues and successes to fade into the background. Meanwhile, welfare state detractors—never in short supply—ensure that its failures, costs, and limits are kept at the forefront of public attention.

Welfare state critics draw on powerfully compelling ideologies. Free-market liberals ground their proposals in a philosophy of freedom, a celebration of market processes, and a critique of state power. Conservatives mobilize ideas of family, community, and charitable giving. Socialists stand for collectivism, equality, and social justice.

What does the welfare state stand for? As it turns out, the creators of the welfare state embraced a range of ideals—Bismarck was a conservative, Beveridge and Keynes were liberals, Atlee and Bevan were democratic socialists, FDR was a pragmatic populist from a patrician background, and the architects of Sweden's welfare state were trade unionists. Few of them were sworn enemies of capitalism or radical opponents of family values. They fought for a welfare state because they were troubled by recurring evidence of economic instability, uncertainty, market failures, family breakdown, domestic squalor, and the hardship and disasters that capitalism brings in its wake. Their case always rested on an appreciation of real world problems and the need for practical amelioration, not utopian visions or radical ideals.

The welfare state is a damage-limiting, problem-solving device rather than anyone's ideal social relationship. Progressives complain it is too mean, too controlling, and too moralizing; that it is a poor substitute for a radical redistribution of wealth and property. Conservatives argue that it is too generous and insufficiently disciplinary; that it undermines enterprise, demoralizes recipients, and creates an overbearing, tax-and-spend state. Welfare recipients insist that they would prefer to have a decent-paying job and bridle at the humiliations associated with means-tested benefits. Taxpayers complain that they work hard to bear the costs of those who do not work. And on it goes.

Conceived in these terms, the best welfare is no welfare at all. And if markets, families, and communities could be made to work of their own accord, there would be no need—and little demand—for welfare state solutions. But in the real world of market failure, family dysfunction, and capitalism's creative destruction, welfare states are nothing short of indispensable.

The indispensable welfare state

Welfare states continue to be a fundamental feature of the world in which we live. In the aftermath of the 2008 Crash, as governments alternated between stimulus and austerity in an effort to revive their economies, and as people took to the streets to protest against cuts to public services and social benefits, 'the social question' once again topped the political agenda. And the social question—how to regulate market capitalism so as to produce a necessary minimum of social security, social integration, and social justice—is, in contemporary societies, chiefly answered by the welfare state.

This book revisits the profound social questions that market capitalism has always raised—the problems of insecurity, inequality, and instability produced by capital accumulation and market processes. And it revisits the political responses to these questions that gave rise, seventy or eighty years ago, to the welfare state. These basic problems are as pressing today as they have ever been, as the Crash and Great Recession vividly demonstrated. But disastrous as the 2008 crisis of global capitalism has been for millions of people, it did not produce the economic and political collapse that characterized the 1930s nor did it give rise to mass movements challenging the democratic state. Among the reasons we were spared these fates, the most important is the existence of welfare states and the protections they provide.

The economic and political catastrophes of the 1930s and 1940s prompted post-war governments to make welfare states a foundation of their nation-states and to build an international monetary system that facilitated that goal. In doing so, they created a structure designed to protect the great mass of working people against the social and economic hazards of unrestrained capitalism—a structure that embodied progressive values of social justice and solidarity as well as a more conservative concern for stability and security. That institutional structure is with us still though we easily forget how essential it is to our way of life. Welfare states may be the indispensable foundation upon which modern capitalist democracies depend; but that doesn't stop opponents trying to dispense with them.

This book explains how these institutions emerged, what they have subsequently become, the challenges they now face, and how they will likely look in the years ahead.

Chapter 2
Before the welfare state

Welfare states are distinctive sets of socio-economic arrangements and styles of governing that emerged in western nations at the end of the 19th century and were fully established in the middle decades of the 20th. But collective social provision in one form or another has been characteristic of societies throughout human history. Viewed in the long term, the welfare state is the latest chapter in an ongoing relationship between economic action and social provision.

Libertarian critics of the welfare state look back nostalgically to the laissez-faire, free-market world of the 19th century and talk of these arrangements as if they were the natural condition of mankind. They view the 'self-regulating market' as the original state of nature and 'government interference' as largely illegitimate and counter-productive. But in the broad sweep of history, 19th-century laissez-faire capitalism was very much an exceptional case. And far from being natural or spontaneous, free-market economic arrangements had to be forcibly established by government action that overturned customary laws, set aside traditional safeguards, and abolished long-standing rights of common.

Pre-capitalist societies did not have distinct 'economies' that were set apart and organized according to a purely economic logic of profit and loss. They did not regard market exchanges as transactions that ought to be governed solely by the laws of supply and demand. Nor did they treat labour power as a marketable commodity distinct from the human being who labours or from the social context in which labour is undertaken. Production and exchange were instead embedded in and constrained by religious, moral, and social rules that limited exploitation and protected against starvation in times of dearth or famine.

To point to these protections and restraints is not to romanticize the pre-capitalist past as some Merrie England idyll of mutual care and support. Pre-modern social arrangements were neither equitable nor democratic and the coming of free trade, free markets, and free labour was, for the commercial classes and their allies, a liberating escape from a world dominated by narrow special interests. But for all their commitment to inherited privilege and status hierarchies, pre-capitalist societies always insisted that economic action be subject to social and moral restraint.

The coming of full-fledged market capitalism in 19th-century Britain was the first time in human history that economic actors shrugged off these social constraints and persuaded the nation's rulers to entrust collective welfare to the logic of private accumulation. The creation of laissez-faire capitalism was, in that respect, an economic and social revolution—a radical departure from the long-term pattern of socially regulated production and exchange. And as the economic historian Karl Polanyi explained, it was the widespread reaction *against* this revolution—and against the dislocations and protests that followed in its wake—that led to the formation of welfare states.

The creation of welfare states in the 20th century was not the beginning of an era in which social protections overlaid and interrupted economic processes; nor a turning away from the natural order of untrammelled commerce. It was the resumption, albeit in a distinctively modern form, of a near-universal pattern that had been pulled apart by the shattering emergence of free-market capitalism.

The social roots of welfare

Why don't human societies allow the poor to starve and the weak to go to the wall? The answer has less to do with altruism, religious belief, and human sympathy—though they certainly play a part—and more to do with the facts of human coexistence and the power relations to which they give rise. In any social organization, social groups are linked together by ties of interdependence. Masters and slaves, lords and vassals, landlords and tenants, employers and employees, states and subjects, men and women—are each interconnected and interdependent. These relations are unequal and exploitative, to be sure, but they tie group fates together in consequential ways. Powerful elites learn that it is in their interests to preserve those they dominate, if only to ensure the regular extraction of tax, labour, or military service; to limit the ravages of disease and the spread of epidemics; and to head off riots and insurrection. Close examination of the ongoing social arrangements of any social grouping generally reveals these complex exchanges and involvements.

Machiavelli advised that a prince who would maintain his state must keep the body politic in security and good health. But the same prudential rules apply within every community and every family. Powerless young children are dependent on their parents but these parents grow old and become dependent in their turn. Those who can work provide for others who cannot, trusting that they will be taken care of when their time comes. Reciprocity extends across generations. Positive emotions of love and affection, solidarity and fellow feeling, altruism and gratitude, are fostered within these interdependencies, translating social necessities into cultural mores and ethical norms. But intertwined with altruistic sentiment are the tougher bonds of mutual need.

These considerations explain why social provision always has multiple sources and is entangled with a variety of relationships. There is always a 'mixed economy' of welfare, with the needs of individuals and households being provided by some combination of kin and community; property and work; church and charity; and local and central state. Their relative importance varies across societies, but there is always a mix—and that continues to be true today, even in societies with extensive welfare states.

Anthropologists describe how tribal societies organized themselves around gift-giving and 'prestation': patterns of extended reciprocity in which gifts would be presented to other groups with whom trade or marital relations existed—often in lavish ceremonies of feasting and display. These acts of giving, receiving, and returning were economically important, distributing material goods to members of the groups involved. But gifts also functioned to build connections and solidarities, to establish relations of power and prestige, and to mark out the structure of social relations in ways that defined these groups and held them together.

Reciprocity is the rule that applies between equals, beneficence the rule connecting superiors and inferiors. To give in expectation of return—either immediately or at some future date—is a relatively simple transaction but the giving of gifts, alms, or largesse is more complex. In most cultures beneficence is the duty of those who can afford it: a social obligation reinforced by motives such as signalling superiority, displaying kingly style, obeying public opinion, affirming ideals, and observing religious duties. In every society the social relations formed by reciprocity and beneficence work to sustain social and economic life, reproduce hierarchy, and hold groups together.

These themes found clear expression in the very different worlds of classical antiquity and medieval Europe where wealthy individuals, notables, and political leaders gave gifts to their city, to their church, and to the common people. In ancient Rome, the institution of 'eurgetism' dictated that wealthy individuals should donate bread and circuses—as well as monuments, civic buildings, and public amenities—as marks of prestige, generosity, and patriotism. And even if the welfare of the poor was not especially valued in Roman culture, poor people benefited from this largesse along with other citizens.

Later, when the Christian church declared the poor 'blessed' and made charity a virtue, almsgiving became a broader social imperative and the practice of pious benevolence spread through the social ranks. Throughout the Middle Ages and the Early Modern period the church—and its network of monasteries, hospitals, and lay fraternities—served as a great engine of redistribution, amassing tithes, taxes, and collections and donating part of the proceeds to the poor. Here too, the non-reciprocal relation between donor and recipient was balanced by non-material returns—in this case gratitude, deference, and the promise of spiritual salvation. One sees similar patterns in Judaism and in the Islamic world.

The obligation to give succour, to assist others, and to be hospitable, was a very general one though it had its limits. The poor of other cities or other faiths, the marginal or unconnected, often found themselves outside the scope of beneficence. And being voluntary (to a degree), such arrangements were subject to the vicissitudes of personal inclination and could not easily cope with large-scale disasters. But mutual aid, charity, and social provision were nevertheless vital features of pre-industrial societies.

These ancient social themes still figure in our own societies today. Even in the most developed welfare states, care-giving is freely undertaken in families; friends and neighbours provide mutual aid; and voluntarism and philanthropy run alongside state welfare, supplementing it at every turn. Nowadays, however, aspects of these practices that were once overt—largesse as a sign of superiority, charity as a sacred duty, bread and circuses as a strategy of rule, welfare as a political *quid pro quo*—persist in less obvious ways, buried in the foundations of our institutions or emerging now and then in popular attitudes towards them.

The expanding role of the state

Social provision is a collective good, necessary to social integration and social order. So it falls to the group's rulers—its elders, chiefs, religious authorities, or government officials—to ensure adequate arrangements are made. In the long process of state formation that began in the late Middle Ages and ultimately gave rise to modern nation-states, the building of institutions for security and welfare played a central role.

As early as the 14th century, the English state had begun to regulate economic life, introducing laws to stabilize employment and provision in the wake of the Black Death. The 16th-century process that historians term 'the Tudor revolution in government' largely consisted of statutes enacted to regulate apprenticeships and labour; control beggars and vagrants; establish rules of 'settlement' (determining the parish to which paupers belonged); set the poor on work; and organize local parishes into a more effective system of poor relief.

These laws, together with customs dating from medieval feudalism, formed the basis of a system of regulation and provision designed to ensure that workers did not starve and that the poor and sick of each parish were cared for. The use of land, the training and employment of labour, the borrowing of money, the formation of contracts, the conduct of markets—all were subject to constraints and limitations. Wages were regulated by guild rules and apprenticeship laws, and the 'just price' for bread and ale was set each year by local Justices of the Peace responsible for ensuring that necessities were available at affordable prices. Labourers and apprentices were lodged and fed in the household of their masters or employers. Grain supplies were monitored to prevent forestalling and hoarding. Land was held not as private property but in a form of stewardship that gave tenants rights of grazing and gleaning, access to common fields and other rights of common. Economic production, master–servant relations, and market exchange were folded into a social fabric of moral rules, religious duties, and customary obligations. And if these norms broke down, as they frequently did, riots and popular protests would often ensue.

As well as regulating the social obligations of economic actors, the early modern English state established a system of relief that came to be known as 'the Poor Law'. Beginning in the late 16th century, Parliament enacted statutes designed to modify the system of religious doles and arrange it on a more uniform, secular basis. Alms previously provided by local churches, monasteries, and charitable hospitals were now distributed by local government officials—the 'overseers of the poor'—and funded by taxes levied on parish householders. Responsibility for indigent individuals remained with families, but where kin could not meet their needs, the government charged the local parish with care of the destitute. In discharging these functions, officials distinguished deserving from undeserving and locals from strangers, providing aid to those incapable of work, refusing it to the 'able bodied', and returning vagrants to their parishes of settlement.

Poor relief in Britain remained the responsibility of local authorities until the early 20th century. But from the 16th century onwards the national government increased its involvement, overseeing the law's administration, establishing a census to enumerate and categorize the indigent, and legislating to encourage the creation of institutions that put the poor to work. The relief and regulation of the poor was one of the paths along which the modern state was built: both in Great Britain and also in colonial America where similar poor law institutions were later established.

The end of the old Poor Laws

By the late 18th century, traditional protections were being eroded by market capitalism, urbanization, and industrialization, and by the new conceptions of political economy and possessive individualism that accompanied them. Proponents of the new economy challenged the old relations of protection and dependency, pressing for the commodification of land, labour, and money and for the abolition of laws and customs that stood in the way of market freedom.

Compared to older arrangements where production was primarily for use, where agrarian producers lived close to subsistence, and where the needs of the household set limits to production, the new capitalism was dynamic, expansive, and transformative. And as industrialization got underway and production became increasingly mechanized, merchants sought to sweep away barriers to trade and expand markets for their goods. Mercantilist controls, protectionist tariffs, guild privileges, apprenticeship laws, just prices, paternalistic provision—the whole political economy of pre-capitalist society—were attacked as unnecessary obstructions to production, commerce, and the expanding wealth of nations.

Market capitalism brought about the eclipse of 'moral economy'. Instead of embedding economic processes within social and moral relations, the logic of capitalist development pressed to dis-embed economic activity, freeing it to compete in open markets untrammelled by moral or social constraint. Social regulation was to give way to economic regulation. Production and exchange were to be determined by demand and supply and not by social obligation or status privilege. Commerce was to be shaped not by customary rules and ancient corporate privileges but by individual calculations of utility and private gain. In the new socio-economic order, contract was more relevant than status, individualism displaced community, and the 'economy' was viewed as a self-contained domain that was to be set apart from the social.

As capitalist enterprise expanded its reach, the old institutions of social regulation and protection were abolished or allowed to pass into disuse, thereby stripping away the protective social layers that had encased production and exchange. Property became more fully 'private'; contracts were to be whatever the contracting parties agreed; and labour, land, and money became freely exchangeable goods to be bought and sold at whatever price the market would bear. To capitalist entrepreneurs, commercial traders, and their middle class supporters, this was a liberating release from restrictive government and the power of special interests. To paternalist landlords, farmworkers, small tenants, and a growing class of wage labourers, it was the demoralization and dehumanization of economic life.

The final chapter in the passing of England's paternalist society is encapsulated in the rise and fall of a poor relief system known as 'Speenhamland' (after the town in which it was originally devised). Introduced in 1795 by Berkshire magistrates during a period of dearth and food riots brought on by the Napoleonic wars, but persisting long after the emergency had passed, Speenhamland was a system of allowances and grants-in-aid of wages designed to enable labourers to feed their families when wages were low and bread expensive. (By 1795, food prices were no longer fixed and the annual assizes of bread and ale had passed into memory, so instead of regulating wages and prices to ensure subsistence as these traditional arrangements had done, Speenhamland sought to ensure subsistence without resorting to direct market controls.) The effect of the system—which soon spread to other rural areas—was, by general agreement, a disaster. The availability of allowances for employed labourers led employers to depress wages, thereby pauperizing their workers (who were put in constant need of poor relief) and threatening to bankrupt local householders whose property taxes funded the system.

Speenhamland was by no means typical and many of its worst effects were soon offset. But it became a by-word for the perversity of paternalistic provision in the new market age. The outrage it provoked fuelled calls for the abolition of the Poor Laws: a demand that claimed support from the ideas of Adam Smith, David Ricardo, and Thomas Malthus, though no political economist fully embraced such a radical position. A Royal Commission of Inquiry, appointed in 1832, produced its Report two years later, documenting the alarming extent of the new pauperism and the ineffectiveness of the system supposed to address it.

Despite the Report's thoroughgoing critique, the old Poor Laws were not altogether abolished. No government could go that far. But the Poor Law Amendment Act of 1834 went a good way towards minimizing social protection and maximizing market freedom. Under the terms of the Act, relief was offered on much more restrictive terms. The new law swept away the poor man's traditional right of parish relief. All 'outdoor relief' was abolished—not just wage supplements to the able bodied but doles to anyone, however infirm or unfit to work—and in its place was established the 'workhouse test.' Anyone wishing to claim relief had to be prepared to enter the workhouse—a closed, disciplinary institution with a regime designed to be 'less eligible' (less attractive) than the meanest conditions of life experienced by wage-earners outside (see Figure 1). The workhouse test became a self-acting measure of destitution since only the truly desperate would choose to enter (see Box 2).

The reaction against laissez-faire

The New Poor Law of 1834 was the embodiment of a newly liberalized market society, stripped of customary protections. The labour market was to be free from outside interference; wages and prices were to be set by market processes; property taxes and public responsibility for welfare were to be minimized; and poor relief was designed to deter all but the truly destitute.

22

1. The women's dining room, St Pancras Workhouse, London (1897).

Box 2 The New Poor Law principles

'The first and most essential of all conditions, a principle which we find universally admitted, even by those whose practice is at variance with it, is that [the pauper's] situation on the whole shall not be made really or apparently so eligible as the situation of the independent labourer of the lowest class'...and...'all relief whatever to able-bodied persons, or to their families, otherwise than in well-regulated workhouses...shall be declared unlawful, and shall cease...'

Report of the Poor Law Commissioners xxvii (1834) at pages 228 and 261

But this laissez-faire utopia quickly ran up against its human limitations and anti-social effects. When the Commission of Inquiry sent out questionnaires to local parish overseers, commissioners were appalled to discover the existence of a huge population of paupers. But this ought not to have surprised them. By the 1830s, two historic processes had long been transforming the condition of the poor: (i) the moral economy of the pre-capitalist world had collapsed and with it the old social protections upon which the poor relied, while (ii) the Industrial Revolution was dislocating the lives of millions of labourers and their families, creating a whole new class of paupers. Between 1750 and 1850, the shift to mechanized farming spurred a massive migration from the countryside to the towns, where the expansion of trade and industry promised work—albeit precarious, casual work—for displaced farm workers. And whereas access to land and community support had allowed the rural poor to eke out a living even in times of want, the new urban proletariat had few resources to help them survive the periodic unemployment characteristic of industrial capitalism.

The living conditions which workers endured in industrial cities were a threat to public health and a moral affront to a nation that considered itself civilized. Conditions in mines and factories were even worse, and affected women and young children as well as men. Parish workhouses in the larger towns and cities struggled to cope with masses of workers thrown out of work by market downturns and by events such as the Irish famine or the collapse of the Lancashire cotton industry. In the face of these pressures, local relief officers relaxed their rules and supplied outdoor relief and public works. Twenty years after the 1834 Act, more than four-fifths of paupers were receiving outdoor relief.

By the middle of the 19th century, the laissez-faire revolution was being challenged by a broad counter-movement of collectivist developments and new social protections. Craftsmen formed craft unions, friendly associations, and mutual aid societies. Voluntary action and private philanthropy expanded. And towards the end of the century, when the laws restricting 'combinations' had been relaxed, unskilled workers organized themselves into unions and used their new power to press for higher wages.

Even as they maintained their free-market creed, British governments recognized 'exceptional circumstances' where protective measures were necessary and laissez-faire principles should be set aside. The regulation of factories, mines, and railways; the provision of public education; the promotion of public health and much else besides were areas that justified central government intervention. City governments did even more: providing clean water, sewers, and sanitation; regulating housing; providing public washhouses, libraries, and parks; and creating a form of 'municipal socialism' that stood in stark contrast to free-market principles.

This historical dialectic is what Polanyi famously called the 'double movement'. On one side, the triumphant forces of laissez-faire liberalism, building a new society based on market freedom, private interest, and a minimal state; on the other, a widespread, diffuse reaction prompted by the pragmatic collectivism of various authorities who took steps to cope with emergencies, repair market failures, and manage the social upheavals caused by the capitalist juggernaut. In the USA, a similar process unfolded: an ideological commitment to laissez-faire and market individualism being offset by public welfare laws at the local level and large-scale disaster relief periodically doled out by the federal authorities.

The paradoxical result was that the 19th-century heyday of individualism and laissez-faire also saw the emergence of a centralized administrative state and municipal socialism. By the end of the century, the question of social provision was caught up in a struggle between two opposing principles: the logic of free-market liberalism *versus* the logic of moral economy and social protection. More than 100 years later, these two competing principles still lie at the heart of our political debates.

Chapter 3
Birth of the welfare state

With remarkable rapidity, a new form of social and economic
government was established throughout the developed world in
the middle decades of the 20th century. An embryonic version
appeared in Germany in the 1880s when Chancellor Bismarck
enacted the first social insurance laws. A decade later,
governments in Denmark, New Zealand, and Australia launched
the first old age pension schemes. In the early 1900s, Liberal
governments in Britain introduced workmen's compensation,
old age pensions, labour exchanges, and a fledgling system of
National Insurance for sickness, invalidity, and unemployment
(see Figure 2).

By the 1930s, the new techniques of government had crossed
the Atlantic to the USA, where President Roosevelt responded
to the Great Depression first with a massive public works
programme and then with the 'New Deal' legislation that
established the American welfare state. In the midst of World
War II the British government and the Provisional Government
of the French Republic published ambitious welfare state
plans and in the post-war years the new welfare states were
everywhere expanded and consolidated. By 1960, every
developed nation had a core of welfare state institutions and
every government had accepted responsibility for managing
the economy. In a remarkably short period, the welfare state

THE DAWN OF HOPE.

Mr. LLOYD GEORGE'S National Health Insurance Bill provides for the insurance of the Worker in case of Sickness.

Support the Liberal Government
in their policy of
SOCIAL REFORM.

Published by the LIBERAL PUBLICATION DEPARTMENT (in connection with the National Liberal Federation and the Liberal Central Association), 42, Parliament Street, Westminster, S.W., and Printed by the National Press Agency Limited, Whitefriars House, London, E.C.
LEAFLET No. 2383.]   28/6/11.   [Price 5s. per 1000.

2. 'The dawn of hope'. National Insurance against sickness and disablement, *Liberal Publication Department* (1911).

had become what political scientist Harold Wilensky described as 'one of the great structural uniformities of modern society' (see Figure 3).

The new welfare states varied, of course. They differed in ways that reflected each nation's history of social provision, its religious

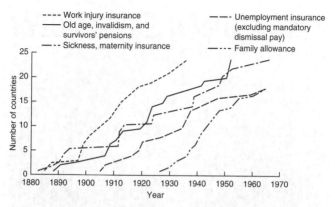

< legend>
--- Work injury insurance
— Old age, invalidism, and survivors' pensions
—·— Sickness, maternity insurance
—— Unemployment insurance (excluding mandatory dismissal pay)
···· Family allowance
</>

3. The diffusion of income maintenance programmes.

traditions, the character of its state, and the political coalitions that shaped its welfare reforms. And in every nation, welfare states had their own legislative histories, involving different constellations of reformers, social movements, political compromises, and legal enactments. But viewed cross-nationally, we glimpse in these stories the presence of large-scale historical processes that were reshaping social, political, and economic landscapes all across the developed world. And once established—as they were, everywhere, by the 1960s—these new welfare states were embraced by all the mainstream political parties (see Box 3).

> ### Box 3 The welfare state becomes indispensable
>
> 'Should any political party attempt to abolish social security, unemployment insurance, and eliminate labor laws and farm programs, you would not hear of that party again in our political history.'
>
> *Republican President Eisenhower, 1954*

To account for this generalized, developmental outcome we need a general, developmental explanation—a set of social dynamics and circumstances that were common to all the western nations at that historical moment. Such an explanation is wide-ranging and multi-dimensional but at its heart is a simple sociological truth: welfare state government emerged as a functional response to the problems of urban, industrial, market societies—above all, to the new risks and insecurities generated by untrammelled market capitalism.

This chapter sketches the historical circumstances and collective actions that produced the new welfare states. I illustrate this international story using details from British and American history but readers should bear in mind that other national histories produced welfare states that differed from these—as Chapter 5 describes.

The hazards of industrial society

At the start of the 20th century, the nations of Western Europe and North America struggled to cope with the disruptions—and what Beveridge termed 'the modern social risks'—brought about by industrialization, urbanization, and rapid population growth. In 1870, one in six western Europeans lived in a town with more than 20,000 inhabitants: by 1910, twice as many did so. Over the same period, the numbers living in large cities of more than 100,000 inhabitants trebled. And in the USA, where a rural to urban migration was already occurring, masses of newly arrived European immigrants crowded into the burgeoning cities.

Mass migration to towns and cities changed how people lived, destabilizing families and setting them adrift from the communities on which they had previously depended. Rapid growth strained amenities and infrastructure, and city governments struggled to cope with expanding needs for housing, transportation, sanitation, water-supply, healthcare, schooling, and poor relief. Nor were these problems confined to the poor. The growth of densely populated cities produced a new interdependence, with poor people's problems spilling over into the lives of the better off. Hazards such as crime and contagious disease threatened rich as well as poor, and the needs of the indigent translated into increased costs for taxpayers. Social life became inescapably collective, with the result that social problems—and their solutions—became collective too. Of all the problems of industrialization, the most insistent was the chronic insecurity of wage labourers. New factories, warehouses, and docks drew people to the towns and gave work to unskilled immigrants and to displaced farmworkers. Urban work was often casual, at-will employment, which left wage labourers exposed to the vicissitudes of the market. As Henry Mayhew observed in his surveys of the London poor, three wet days in a row could bring 30,000 people to the brink of starvation.

The concentration of industry, casual employment, and the cyclical movements of trade generated periodic bouts of mass unemployment, affecting whole segments of the population in a way that agricultural unemployment had rarely done. The frequent result was widespread destitution, concentrated in cities and towns, placing severe strains on poor relief and giving rise to a threatening 'residuum' of impoverished, unemployed men.

New social forces

The historical processes shaping industrial society gave rise to social problems. But they also created social forces with the potential to remedy them. Industrialization concentrated workers in large mines and factories and facilitated the growth of labour organization. Trade union federations appeared, first in Germany and England, but eventually in all developed countries. These were followed by the formation of workers' parties, first in Germany around 1870, then in the other European countries, and finally in Britain, where the British Labour Party was formed in

1900. The workers' new organizational strength shifted the balance of power between social classes, giving labour's representatives a new-found influence.

The emergence of organized labour as an industrial and political force pushed western societies towards a universal franchise, which in turn created new demands for economic security and redistributive policies. By the middle of the 20th century, in one country after another, the labour movement and its allies pressed for social reform and for more egalitarian conceptions of citizenship and its entitlements. These processes are what T. H. Marshall referred to when he argued that democratization led to social rights. And they are what 'power resources' theorists such as Walter Korpi have in mind when they observe that the strength of a nation's welfare state is directly related to the power of its labour movement.

Failures of social provision

The creation of welfare states was prompted by the failure of existing systems of social provision. The depressions of the 1890s and the 1930s made awareness of these failures widespread and urgent but the inability of the old arrangements to cope with urban poverty had long been apparent to those involved. Poor law officials, church leaders, charity workers, labour representatives, and government ministers were all, in their different ways, conscious of the system's problems (see Figure 4). And their misgivings were confirmed by a growing literature that measured the extent of poverty and documented the plight of the poor.

The fundamental problem was that the system of poor laws and local charity was designed to operate in rural society as a means of relieving old, sick, or invalid individuals who were beyond the care of kin. It was a residual system: a supplement to the care-giving of families and an emergency fallback in hard times—and altogether unequal to the problems of industrial, urban society.

4. Soup kitchen in Chicago during the Great Depression (1930).

So long as laissez-faire liberalism was the dominant approach
to policy, reform efforts aimed to shore up the old system and
maintain its basic principles, as when unreconstructed
liberals continued to stress 'self-help' as the antidote to life's
vicissitudes. But anyone familiar with the social question knew
that the hazards of unemployment, illness, and old age could
not be met from savings when work was so poorly paid and
intermittent. And though mutual aid and friendly societies were
widespread, these collective forms of self-help had limits too,
being prone to adverse selection; more effective for routine
accidents than for emergencies; and vulnerable to bankruptcy if
a local industry collapsed or if unpaid officers proved dishonest
or incompetent.

Another reform intended to patch up laissez-faire while
maintaining its fundamental axioms was the 'scientific' approach

to charitable giving pioneered by the Charity Organization Society (COS)—an association founded in London in 1869 and soon spreading to cities across Britain and the USA. Scientific charity stressed the need for classification, for careful differentiation between deserving and undeserving, and the importance of personal visiting and reformatory casework. Above all, it deplored the evils of 'indiscriminate alms giving'—a practice that, according to the COS, served to demoralize the mendicant poor while increasing their number.

This emphasis on reformatory interventions by trained case-workers would later form a hallmark of the social work profession that developed within the welfare state, but in its 19th-century context, the COS approach was no match for the problems it addressed. Like the Poor Law workhouses whose principles it shared, the sheer volume of need periodically overwhelmed scientific charity's efforts. And like the workhouses and their badges of pauperism, the stern agents of the COS were heartily disliked by those they sought to help.

By the 1890s, it was increasingly apparent that the majority of those in poverty were poor through no fault of their own, having been rendered destitute by casual employment and bread-line wages. As the shadow of blame was lifted, the austere logic of the Poor Law and the COS was more and more brought into question. Faced with the problems of industrial society, existing solutions exhibited the wrong structure and operated at the wrong scale. The old forms of charity had operated alongside a rural paternalism that assumed strong communities and common access to land—all of which were now things of the past. The principles of 1834 insisted that able-bodied men could always find sustaining work if they wanted to: a dogma that was no longer credible. Philanthropy was sporadic and not uniformly available; the demographics of need and the geography of giving were often mismatched; and in times of crisis charitable doles were soon overwhelmed.

Public and private relief had traditionally been organized at the local level, where people knew one another and communities looked after their own. But as the 1909 Poor Law Report observed, labour markets and unemployment were increasingly national phenomena and would more appropriately be dealt with by a national agency—such as the new Ministry of Labour that the Report proposed. As the scale of the problems increased, only national government could provide adequate solutions. Local relief, private charity, and efforts to improve individual character would eventually give way to national arrangements, organized and funded by the state using techniques designed to address structural problems at an appropriate level.

New recipes for action

When old arrangements are seen to falter, new ideas quickly emerge. Beginning in the 1880s and 1890s, British thinkers such as T. H. Green and L. T. Hobhouse and Americans such as Lester Frank Ward reworked the tenets of political liberalism, proposing a more positive vision of the state, and reconceptualizing the relationship between social and economic policy. Expansive ideas of freedom and citizenship, more social conceptions of rights and justice, new understandings of economic processes, and the powerful new technology of social insurance (see Box 4) all took shape in this period, each one predicated on the failures of laissez-faire and envisioning institutions that might replace them.

This 'new liberalism'—like the Progressive movement that took off in the USA at the same time—insisted that individual freedom was best fostered not by leaving people to their own devices but by securing for them the education, welfare, and security needed to exercise real autonomy. Social imperialists and eugenicists, disturbed by the 'degenerate' condition of city-dwellers and army recruits, insisted that population fitness was vital to the nation's economic and military success, and that this ought not to be left to blind chance or market forces. And throughout Europe, socialist

Box 4 Social insurance: a new power to serve mankind

'There is an exhilaration in the study of insurance questions because there is a sense of elaborating new and increased powers which have been devoted to the service of mankind...we bring the magic of averages to the aid of the millions.'

Winston Churchill, introducing National Insurance legislation in 1911

thought won converts, both in its revolutionary versions—which had strong support in trade unions and social democratic parties—and in more moderate versions, such as the Fabian movement which flourished in Britain (and briefly in the USA) and which urged gradual collective action as the cure for capitalism's ills.

These intellectual currents differed from one another and appealed to different audiences. But they shared a common conviction that the laissez-faire and localist conceptions lying at the heart of 19th-century liberalism were no longer viable. In the Victorian era local government had been called on to solve the problems of the towns and cities—and had responded by creating the 'gas and water socialism' of places like Birmingham and Manchester and the 'machine politics' welfare of Chicago and Boston. In the 20th century it was to the national state (or federal government) that such calls were increasingly addressed.

State capacity

The welfare state is an apparatus of social administration through which the state assumes some level of control over social and economic processes. In much of the developed world, the state capacity and competence needed for effective action of this kind had started to emerge by the beginning of the 20th century. By the end of the two World Wars it was becoming firmly established.

In Britain, state power had been slowly growing since the 16th century, but it surged during the 19th century when problems of industrial society came to be seen as the responsibility of national government. In one area after another—factories, mines, child labour, public health, prisons—a public outcry about some newly discovered social evil prompted government investigations. These inquires would render the problem more visible, generating demands for more public action. Over time, officials developed expertise, put in place standards, created inspectorates; and eventually established new departments of state (such as the Board of Health, the Factory Inspectorate, the Poor Law Commission, or the Prison Commission) charged with managing the problem.

By the 1870s, the UK government was maintaining paupers; limiting the employment of women and children; financing and supervising schools, reformatories, prisons, and police forces; and enforcing compulsory vaccinations. Municipal town councils were doing even more. The Victorian state—despite its laissez-faire principles and the Treasury's efforts to minimize expenditure—was already an activist, social policy state. In America, public welfare institutions grew along with the towns and cities, assembling an extensive state apparatus at the local level. So although federalist arrangements slowed the growth of national power, at least until the New Deal, American government also amassed new powers and competences that were at odds with the country's liberal, laissez-faire orthodoxies.

By the early decades of the 20th century national governments across the developed world had enacted social insurance, income tax, old age pensions, and child welfare laws, creating new administrative networks connecting the central state to the population and to individual workers, firms, and households. By the 1930s, many of the fiscal and administrative innovations on which welfare states depend had been tried out and state officials had proven capable of administering them. By the 1940s, the experience of two World Wars had greatly expanded the reach of state regulation, planning, and the direction of supplies and production, demonstrating the ability of governments to mobilize populations and run economies.

These developments produced an enhanced sense of the power of state action and a new belief in its desirability. Wartime governments had managed economies, created emergency services, and actively shaped public morale. In the years after 1945, civil servants and government ministers began to plan how these extensive powers of government might be put to work in peacetime.

Catalysing events

Major institutional change—such as the emergence of a new mode of government—is a rare event and one that generally takes place in the wake of crisis or disruption. And indeed the emergence of welfare states was prompted by momentous events that made structural reform appear both possible and necessary.

First in the Depression of the 1890s and then more decisively after the Wall Street Crash of 1929, international trade broke down, producing mass unemployment, runaway inflation, and radical political movements. In the 1930s, democratic governments collapsed, ushering in Fascist and Nazi regimes, expanding the appeal of the communist movement, and igniting a six-year conflagration that left Europe in ruins. In 1918, the victorious nations had hastened back to their pre-war economic policies, re-establishing the orthodoxies of free trade, the Gold Standard, and minimum public spending. By 1945, these orthodoxies had been utterly discredited. Following the economic collapse of the 1930s and the bloody turmoil that followed, few believed in laissez-faire and politicians everywhere embraced the need to stabilize markets and assure full employment. Capitalists too acknowledged the benefits of corporatist agreements and more managed economies, just as they acceded to the new system of currency and capital controls established at Bretton Woods.

The events of these years shifted the balance of political power and the character of social relations, increasing the influence of trade unions and working people. America's New Deal recognized the legal standing of organized labour, established employee rights, and opened the way to a more powerful union movement. During World War II, the British government had sought trade union cooperation in redirecting industrial production and averting the damaging strikes that had occurred during the previous war—a development that significantly enhanced the power of labour. And as the war against Germany wore on, governments sought to boost troop and civilian morale by promising that the return of peace would usher in an era of social reform and social justice (see Figure 5).

Mobilizing for war changed the combatant nations. Rulers in wartime have always tried to ensure the loyalty of their militaries—Civil War Veterans Pensions in 19th-century America are a case in point, as is the GI Bill of 1944. But in total war national leaders also had to win the commitment of masses of civilians and the promise of large-scale social reform was an important means to this end. Total war brought social classes closer together. Enemy bombs fell on rich as well as poor, and the evacuation of city children to the countryside revealed the squalor in which many of the urban poor lived. Wartime social services—such as Britain's Emergency Hospital Service or provision for the victims of air attacks—provided the same benefits to all individuals, regardless of ability to pay. War also made the population's health a political concern, with the remarkable result that after years of UK government food rationing average levels of health and nutrition actually improved. In these years of shared adversity and common sacrifice a more egalitarian society was born, so when war's end finally came,

5. 'Here's to the brave new world'. Cartoon by Illingsworth, *Daily Mail* (1942).

nations set about the work of social and economic reconstruction with a new sense of idealism and energy (see Figure 6).

But as always, idealism had a materialistic corollary. Economic collapse and total war had changed perceptions of social risk, making the middle classes feel vulnerable to the hazards of market society. Prior to the 1930s, welfare policy was aimed at the poor and relief was usually meagre and stigmatizing. After the 1930s,

Full Employment
in a
Free Society

A Summary by
Sir WILLIAM BEVERIDGE

Published by the New Statesman and Nation and Reynolds News

6D.

6. 'Full employment in a free society', by William Beveridge (1944).

welfare policy was aimed at the middle classes as well, with the consequence that it fundamentally changed its character. Henceforth, social policy would be more universal in its reach and less stingy in its provision; and economic policy would aim to manage markets and their outcomes rather than simply set them free.

Coalitions for reform

Welfare states were functional solutions to the problems of industrial capitalism. But they had to be built. And the political leaders who built them—together with civil servants, expert advisers, and social reformers—belonged to various parties, were possessed of diverse ideologies, and pursued multiple objectives.

By the 1940s, the need for new institutions of economic management and social provision was broadly accepted. And although there were fierce debates about the design of the new arrangements—with trade unionists pressing for tax-funded benefits rather than flat-rate contributions and socialists objecting to 'palliatives' that would prevent more fundamental change—a range of political forces took part in their creation. Welfare states are sometimes seen as an achievement of the industrial working classes but they mostly came about through broad coalitions representing farmers, middle classes, and professionals as well. And the most extensive, most durable welfare states are generally those that serve the interests of the broadest and most powerful coalitions.

If political actors were diverse, so too were their motives. In the aftermath of Fascism, European leaders sought to bind their middle classes to the democratic state by offering social provision that would benefit the better off as well as the poor. But the working classes had to be won over too, not least because the Depression and the War had increased the appeal of communism and Soviet propaganda held out state socialism as a better prospect for working people.

Reformers of all parties combined high-minded moral purpose with more partisan motivation. Welfare payments were given as a matter of social justice—but they were also made in exchange for votes, or loyalty to the state, or for the avoidance of trouble. Transfer payments were made to promote equality—but they could also uphold status hierarchies and income differentials. Social welfare was made to humanize capitalism—but also to make it more resistant to socialist challenge. Social provision was made to enable citizenship and positive liberty—but also to counteract 'degeneration' and improve what policymakers feared was an increasingly unfit race. And benefits were paid to secure workers and their families—but also to stimulate demand, keep money circulating, prompt investment, and sustain commerce. Welfare states have always been about economic efficiency as well as social equity, serving the interests of rulers as well as the needs of the ruled.

To be 'for' the welfare state in the 1940s was not—nor is it today—to be on the side of the angels. It was to be in favour of the social control of economic processes (with all the political conflict and administrative challenges which that involves) rather than in favour of entrusting these processes to the private choices of individual entrepreneurs, multi national corporations, or financial speculators.

Nor did being 'for' the welfare state mean being 'against' capitalism. As the economist John Maynard Keynes observed, welfare states were not a means of destroying capitalist market processes; they were a set of collective action techniques for its more efficient management (see Box 5)—which is why businessmen and industrialists did not more vigorously resist these developments and often actively supported them.

Employers in different countries and different industries varied in their reactions. American employers fought to preserve wage inequalities, promote company-based welfare, and suppress

Box 5 Saving capitalism

'[Keynes] detested the inefficiency of unregulated capitalism only less than he dreaded the waste and suffering of a proletarian revolution . . . he therefore made it his life's work to save capitalism by altering its nature.'

Kingsley Martin, The New Statesman 1946

unions. Swedish employers did the opposite. But employers everywhere saw the need for social insurance and regarded the health, welfare, and education of workers as assets to their firms. Welfare states met the non-market needs of market capitalism—supplying the social arrangements and human capacities upon which economic activity depended—and the more far-seeing capitalists understood and embraced this.

The welfare states that took shape in the post-war decades differed, as I've said. Some—such as America—provided little more than the minimum of insurance coverage, social welfare, and economic management that was dictated by the functional requisites of modern social organization and the non-market needs of capitalist markets. Others—most famously Sweden and the Nordic nations—were much more egalitarian and solidaristic. Nations such as Britain developed social insurance schemes based on universalistic principles, with everyone paying the same flat-rate contributions and receiving the same flat-rate benefits. Germany, Austria, and France, by contrast, linked contribution and benefit levels to earnings, thereby ensuring that labour market differentials were reproduced in the costs and benefits of welfare. Strongly centralized states such as France and Britain empowered central government agencies to administer the system; federal nations with weaker states—most notably the USA—devolved many of these tasks to local government. Yet other nations, such as the Netherlands and Germany, relied on churches and voluntary associations to deliver social services.

Governments in Germany, France, and Sweden established corporatist arrangements that enlisted employer federations and trade unions as 'social partners' to modernize industry, train workers, ensure full employment, and control inflation. By contrast, US and UK governments made minimal use of planning or corporate agreements and relied on easing consumer credit or fostering market forces as means to growth and prosperity. Nordic welfare states established public childcare and support for the elderly, thereby increasing the autonomy and the equality of women. Nations such as Italy, Germany, and France aimed to preserve traditional family structures and concentrated on the needs of the industrial male worker.

Each welfare state was, in these respects, distinctive. But for all these differences of detail, the fundamental fact of welfare state development was an event of international dimensions and a universal characteristic of capitalist democracies in the post-war world.

Chapter 4
The welfare state 1.0

The creation of full-fledged welfare states was part of the massive reconstruction undertaken by war-torn European nations in the years after 1945. And during the decades of growth that followed, a commitment to the welfare state became the settled principle around which a lasting political consensus took shape. In the USA, New Deal institutions formed the basis for a parallel settlement that likewise endured until the 1970s and beyond.

In these post-war decades a new mode of government came into being. Its specific forms varied: Britain's *Welfare State*, *L'Etat Providence* in France, the Dutch *Verzorgingsstaat*, Germany's *Sozialstaat*, America's *New Deal*, and Sweden's *Folkhemmet* all had unique characteristics of their own. But these newly-emergent welfare states shared a distinctive set of features that marked them off from the old poor laws on the one side and from state socialism on the other. It is these defining features that I want to identify here.

The fledgling welfare states of the 1880s and 1900s had pioneered social insurance but their actual policies involved laws of limited reach and relatively modest expenditures. In the 1950s and 1960s, welfare states expanded in scope and ambition, becoming vast machines for economic growth and social governance, deploying a myriad of laws and regulations, and spending between 20 and 30 per cent of GDP. Let's call this first full-fledged version 'Welfare State 1.0' (WS 1.0) and use it to describe how welfare states are structured and as a base line from which to measure subsequent developments.

Welfare state sectors

Welfare states generally have five institutional sectors: (i) social insurance; (ii) social assistance; (iii) publicly funded social services; (iv) social work and personal social services; and (v) economic governance. I will describe these here in the WS 1.0 forms that predominated from the 1940s until the 1980s. In later chapters I discuss how they subsequently changed.

Social insurance against loss of earnings is the cornerstone of the welfare state. It addresses the central problem of capitalist labour markets—the insecurity of wage-workers and their families—by means of a collective risk pooling that indemnifies losses and generalizes security. Beveridge talked of state insurance as 'a new type of human institution' and its emergence does indeed constitute a breakthrough in social and economic governance.

Social insurance programmes are typically state-administered, legally compelled, more or less comprehensive schemes designed to protect workers and their families against loss of earnings due to injury, sickness, old age, disability, or unemployment. They emulate private insurance by requiring the insured to make contributions, specifying the contingencies that trigger benefits, and establishing contractual entitlements. But they differ from private insurance in that they de-link premium levels from risk levels and enrol everyone, regardless of risk profile. These departures are feasible because the insured population is large and diverse and because enrolment is compelled by the state. No private insurance scheme could provide guaranteed coverage of this kind.

In schemes such as National Insurance in the UK or Social Security in the USA, employees are obliged to make regular contributions (supplemented by employer contributions made on their behalf) on the basis of which they are entitled to sickness and disability benefits, unemployment payments, retirement pensions, and so on. The effect of these risk-pooling, forced-savings schemes is to smooth out fluctuations in earnings and consumption, thereby redistributing income across the life-course and across economic cycles. And although these schemes produce some cross-class redistribution—low-paid workers generally benefit more than they contribute—their primary effect is to provide security to everyone in employment, rich as well as poor.

Social insurance schemes are enduringly popular with the public, not least because they have proven effective in reducing hardship among the elderly and the short-term unemployed. The public also favours the benefit-in-exchange-for-contributions character of these schemes and the fact that recipients of insurance benefits are spared the intrusions and stigma that frequently accompany means-tested welfare.

Social assistance (or 'welfare' as it is known in the USA and, increasingly, in the UK) refers to the safety net of non-contributory, income-support programmes that relieve those whose income is insufficient for their basic needs. Welfare state founders such as William Beveridge assumed that the need for such assistance would disappear as the entire workforce came to be insured but subsequent events—particularly the collapse of full employment and the growth of single-parent families—ensured that these programmes have remained important. Many founders also intended assistance to take the form of social rights uniformly available to needy citizens but over time older 'poor law' patterns of discretionary provision have tended to reappear.

Social assistance benefits are typically selective and means-tested, provided only to those who demonstrate need. Examples would be the American programmes of General Assistance, food stamps, Earned Income Tax Credits, Child Tax Credits, Supplementary Security Income, Medicaid, and TANF; or British ones such as 'Income Support' (previously, 'National Assistance' and 'Supplementary Benefits' and currently transitioning to 'Universal Credit'), housing benefits, council tax allowance, rent rebates, free school meals, and means-tested jobseeker's allowance.

Social assistance is funded out of general taxation and is modestly redistributive. It tends to be strongly gendered, its primary recipients being women and children. Of all welfare state programmes, means-tested income support is the least popular with the public and frequently prompts moral panics about work-shy scroungers, irresponsible single parents, and 'benefits tourists'. As historian Michael Katz remarks, 'Nobody likes welfare'. Nevertheless, its programmes remain vital—even in the egalitarian, high-income Nordic countries where between 5 and 10 per cent of families receive such assistance in any year.

Publicly-funded social services provide free (or subsidized) access to goods such as education, healthcare, childcare, public transport, legal aid, and so on. And at the local level, residents enjoy parks, libraries, museums, sports and recreational facilities, affordable housing, and other public amenities, paid for out of local government revenues. Social rights and services thus provide 'decommodified' solutions to problems of urbanization and marketization.

These public services—which are generally the least stigmatizing, most egalitarian aspects of the welfare state—come closest to being the 'social rights' that T. H. Marshall described, being provided as of right and operating outside of the market. Their extent varies across nations but even in a market-oriented system such as the USA, services such as elementary and high school education are provided free of charge and as of right.

Employee rights—minimum wages, paid holidays, parental leave, employment protections, workplace dismissal and promotion procedures, etc.—are also social (or 'economic') rights, as are the right to join a union, the collective right to strike, and so on. The extent of these rights—together with employment services of various kinds—generally reflect the political strength of trade unions.

A fourth sector consists of *social work and personal social services*. In addition to insurance benefits, social assistance, and public services, welfare states provide personalized forms of support such as social work with families, children's services, social care for the elderly, community care for the mentally ill, and probation and aftercare supervision for offenders. Some of these services are straightforward forms of public provision such as childcare or home-based care for the elderly or disabled. But in other instances, social work professionals engage with clients in ways that combine care and control, focusing on families and individuals who have come to the authorities' notice because of some perceived dysfunction or because of claims they make upon the state. The personal social services are the welfare state's response to the problem of failing or dysfunctional families that would otherwise lack community support.

These social work interventions aim to 'normalize' and discipline at the same time that they extend care and support. And they mostly target the same lower-class populations that receive social assistance, with women and children as their primary focus. The French sociologist Jacques Donzelot describes these as so many ways of 'policing the family'—by which he means that families deemed problematic are inspected and pressed to adopt 'normal' patterns of child-rearing, better work habits, more responsible sexual behaviour, and so on. This state-sponsored effort to normalize individuals and families—often couched in the language of psychotherapy and backed by court order—is a modern development but it echoes the pastoral care and religious discipline that flourished after the Reformation and retains some of the moral authoritarianism of that religious heritage. Similarly, the casework methods that lie at the heart of modern social work were, as we saw, pioneered by scientific charities such as the COS.

Donzelot reminds us that welfare states regulate and secure families just as they regulate and secure economies. Indeed, in the early 20th century, many commentators viewed this 'invasion of the home' as the most radical and disturbing aspect of the new welfare state government. Over time, however, the character of social work has changed—not least because families and their presenting problems are constantly evolving—and rather than functioning primarily as a regulatory police, much caseworker time today is devoted to advocating for clients and guiding them through the maze of benefit applications processes.

Finally, there is what might be described as the *government of the economy*. Welfare state programmes depend upon the operation of large-scale government controls on economic life. Nationalization of industry; economic planning; allocation of property rights; tax laws; fiscal policy; monetary policy; consumer credit policy; labour market policies; corporatist agreements; prices and incomes policies; farming and food subsidies; industrial policy; training programmes; regional investment programmes; financial regulations; minimum wage laws—all of these are, or have been, instruments of economic management used in welfare states.

After 1945, governments assumed responsibility for assuring economic growth, curbing booms and slumps, and keeping unemployment and inflation within acceptable levels. And in the decades since, they have shaped the institutions of economic governance (corporatist agreements, associations, labour unions, etc.) and have variously used planning, direct controls, Keynesian, monetarist, supply-side, and neoliberal policy instruments in pursuit of these goals. Governing the economy is the welfare state's answer to the economic problems associated with market capitalism: operating both at the microeconomic level of job training, employment services, and protections and at the macroeconomic level of demand management and money supply. This dimension of the welfare state was highly visible in the post-war era when governments undertook to ensure full employment, both as a right for workers and as an economic underpinning for spending programmes. It has become less explicit in the decades since the 1970s, when governments placed inflation control ahead of full employment and ceded control of interest rates to central banks.

Even in today's neoliberal globalization era, economic governance remains an essential element of welfare states and annual public expenditure budgets still operate as basic tools of economic management. Government social spending has large-scale impacts on national economies, both as tax-funded expenditures and as benefit-fuelled private consumption. And of course welfare states are themselves major job-creators, employing millions of people, a majority of whom are women. In the USA, government jobs account for around 15 per cent of total employment, while the Swedish figure is twice as high. In Britain, the nation's biggest employer is the NHS, which employs 1.7 million people.

There is one other feature of the welfare state landscape I want to highlight, lest it escape our attention. Sometimes called the 'hidden welfare state', it consists of welfare benefits that are channelled through the tax system or else through private employment contracts. The US home-mortgage tax allowance, for example, is a large-scale government welfare and stimulus programme the costs of which are greater than the cost of the nation's public housing. Similarly, corporate welfare schemes (providing enhanced retirement, healthcare, and other 'fringe benefits' to certain employees) are subsidized and regulated by government but provided by employers as a form of tax-exempt compensation. These forms of social provision—the least egalitarian of all—are mostly buried in the tax code and are rarely the focus of political debate.

These, then, are the major sectors of the welfare state complex and the primary instruments of welfare state government. Simultaneously operating at the macro-level of the national economy and the population, and the micro-level of firms, families, and individuals, they function to modify the economic outcomes and social relations that capitalist markets would otherwise create; to secure a politically-defined minimum of social and economic security; and to ensure the socialization and well-being of children, young workers, and individuals.

Functions and dysfunctions

To talk about the functions of the welfare state is not to suggest the absence of conflict or the routine attainment of success. In practice, the sectors operate within different bandwidths of success and failure and all of them 'fail' to some degree. National governments usually have it within their power to establish social insurance, social assistance, and public services with reasonable levels of efficiency. But not all states succeed in doing so. And the ability of states to govern national economies is much less certain, as are their abilities to police families or discipline wayward individuals.

Welfare policies are rarely carried out smoothly because while the relation between the welfare state and market capitalism is functionally *necessary* it is also structurally *contradictory*. In welfare state societies, privately-determined economic action and publicly-determined social protection are shackled together. The result is a contradictory hybrid in which each structure works to sustain but also to undermine the other. Within this arrangement, the welfare state is always the subordinate or ancillary institution rather than the primary one with welfare benefits and transfers being viewed as 'secondary' redistributions that modify a more fundamental, 'primary' distribution grounded in private property and market transactions. The result is that welfare state policies generally stop short of posing major challenges to private property. It also means that the fiscal viability of specific welfare states depends on the ability of their national economies to generate growth and prosperity.

Welfare state government is always a delicate balancing act—a matter of modifying economic outcomes without obstructing enterprise; protecting labour without reducing employment; taxing profits without harming growth or prompting investment strikes; mobilizing government power while checking state overreach and upholding individual liberty. It is also always a regulatory challenge. Welfare states seek to impose social and political controls on economic and family processes that often escape or respond perversely to these regulatory efforts. This fundamental contradiction—which we might describe as the problem of *system-conflict*—ensures that welfare states are often prone to functional difficulties.

A further corollary is the fact that welfare state programmes are generally ameliorative rather than curative. They aim to manage failure and dysfunction rather than offer radical cures—a limitation that exasperates advocates and critics alike. The reason for this is that while welfare programmes moderate insecurity and instability they do not abolish the structural sources of these problems. On the contrary: they *sustain* capitalist markets and private property, even as they seek to make them compatible with socially acceptable outcomes. The result is that problems associated with market failure and maldistribution continually reassert themselves.

A new style of governing

Collective efforts to impose social regulation on economic action have been a feature of societies throughout the course of human history. But there are marked discontinuities in the means whereby this regulation is undertaken. In that long-term story, the emergence of welfare states marked an important new chapter.

When historians describe what was new about the 20th-century welfare state, they point to the abolition of poor laws and their harsh indignities. They point to the emergence of government schemes for organizing labour markets and securing workers' income; and to the increased role of national agencies and the shift of responsibilities from local to national government. They describe how welfare provision became a mainstream process with a majority of citizens laying claim to rights and entitlements. And they note the expanded role that welfare law and social work came to play in the private lives of families and individuals. The welfare state was, they explain, a historic transformation from residualism to universalism, from emergency relief to routine prevention, and from private charity to public welfare.

But the most profound discontinuity marking the welfare state's emergence was not so much these altered practices, important though they were, but instead a fundamental change in the underlying rationality of government. What marked the welfare state off from its predecessors was an altered conception of the nature and purpose of governing and of the character of the objects—above all the economy and the population—to which government action was addressed. Welfare state government was distinguished by a new style of thinking about, and acting upon, the problems of unemployment, insecurity, and uncertainty: an approach that—together with new technologies of social insurance, social provision, and economic regulation—affected the whole economy and population, and proceeded on quite new principles. Today, more than seventy years later, this distinctive style of governing continues to shape how advanced societies govern economic and social life, albeit in forms that continue to evolve and develop.

To explain this altered conception more concretely we can examine how it informed the new style of governing that emerged in Britain—a nation where the shift from laissez-faire liberalism to a welfare state mode of government was especially pronounced.

In the 19th century the teachings of classical political economy insisted that the relation between social protection and economic enterprise was, to speak anachronistically, a zero sum game. Money spent on poor relief was a drag on industry and a disincentive to work; every shilling given to a pauper was a shilling removed from the productive economy; public spending crowded out private spending. Charity and poor law provision should therefore be minimized lest they multiply the poor and worsen the ratio of population to resources.

At the start of the 20th century there was a shift in thinking about government's capacity to manage the economy and about the benefits of so doing. The new economic thinking—subsequently associated with John Maynard Keynes, though he was by no means its only progenitor—regarded unemployment as a 'problem of industry' operating at the level of the labour market as a whole, not as a problem of work effort on the part of individuals. It pointed to the possibility—confirmed by real-world events but long denied in economic theory—that markets could reach equilibrium at low levels of employment and produce prolonged, destructive depressions. It pointed to the positive, multiplier effects that government interventions could create by injecting money into a depressed economy to create employment, buoy up demand, and boost investor confidence. And it pointed to the positive outcomes produced when workers were secured against the risk of economic misfortune. In the world of laissez-faire, raising workers' wages and providing income transfers to the poor had been vices with detrimental economic and social consequences. In the new approach they became virtues that brought economic and social benefits in their wake.

The new welfare state government socialized processes of control and of provision, organized them on a national scale, and made them public responsibilities. Securing employment, sustaining household income, relieving poverty, providing social services, reducing uncertainty—all of these became functions to be undertaken at an aggregate level, harnessing the benefits of scale, the law of large numbers and what Churchill called 'the miracle of averages'. The objects addressed by government came to be the labour market as a whole; the structure of industrial production; and the national economy—the last being understood as a set of macroeconomic relations between aggregates such as national revenue, total consumption, and the total volume of savings and investment. The welfare state was thus made possible by a new form of macroeconomic and macrosociological governance. It was a 'statification' and systematization of governing practices that were previously local, private, and piecemeal. And it was a professionalization and a routinization of interventions that were previously left to volunteers and amateurs.

Where laissez-faire insisted on individualism, competition, and private action, the welfare state stressed cooperation, coordination, and organized collective action—not just as an assertion of values, but as an adaptation to modern social and economic life. Where laissez-faire insisted on minimizing government and freeing up markets, the new approach saw government assume responsibility for managing labour markets and assuring economic outcomes (see Box 6). The use of comprehensive, compulsory, collective action—with the nation state acting upon the population and the economy, the family, and the firm—became the welfare state's signature approach (see Box 7). The result was welfare states that were more comprehensive, more routine, and more systematic than any prior form of social provision, utilizing apparatuses of insurance, risk-management, and regulation that had no historical equivalents.

A new politics

Welfare state programmes had a powerful appeal for western political parties and their electorates in the middle decades of the 20th century. In that era of growth and prosperity, these programmes were extended and improved, enabling governments to provide enhanced benefits to their constituents and supplying voters and union members with material returns for their support. Increased taxation was a cause for complaint, as was the inflationary effect of increased public spending, and new groups frequently emerged pressing new claims and seeking new benefits. But in the post-war decades of growth, these problems were offset by rising wages, rising profits, and rising productivity.

Key to its political strength was the fact that welfare state largesse reached far beyond the poor, bringing benefits to the middle classes and the well-to-do. Programmes such as healthcare, higher education, and the home mortgage tax allowance were a boon to wealthier households. Middle-class women were enabled to undertake higher education and pursue professional careers. Employers enjoyed the benefits of a trained, healthy workforce and worked with unions to secure wage and productivity deals that brought industrial peace, allowed for longer-term planning, and contributed to competitive outcomes. Trade unions in many nations became agents of integration rather than conflict and were rewarded with a seat at the table in matters of economic government. And working people enjoyed the improved security and standards of living delivered by full employment, rising real wages, and improved public provision.

Once established, welfare states generated their own constituencies—particularly among women, middle-class professionals, public employees, and liberal elites—and their own growth dynamic. New benefits became settled entitlements. Improved circumstances led to heightened expectations. Groups that were left out pressed to be included. New social problems were discovered requiring new forms of state action. And an increasingly affluent middle class demanded improved social services, better education, and higher levels of healthcare. For a time, welfare states came to be seen as the solution to every problem and the institutions to which demands for social rights and social justice would automatically be addressed. Governments would discover—when these self-reinforcing growth dynamics became less sustainable—that reversing these developments would be much more difficult.

Chapter 5
Varieties

'The' welfare state does not exist as such. Only particular welfare states exist, each of them different, each of them complex, each of them constantly in motion. I have used the USA and the UK to illustrate the welfare state's history and character but neither of these nations is especially typical. No national welfare state ever is. Looked at in detail, every developed country has a distinctive welfare state of its own.

Welfare states generally rely on the same basic institutions—social insurance, social assistance, public services, and so on—but these institutions can operate in different ways. Unemployment insurance may provide wide eligibility, easy access, and high-level benefits or it may be restrictive and conditional. Public services can be extensive and of high quality or meagre and limited. And programme settings change as circumstances change. When large numbers are out of work for lengthy periods, there will be pressure to extend the duration of unemployment benefits. Conversely, when labour markets are strong, and claimants are viewed as jobless by choice, there will be pressure to restrict benefits. Conflicts over programme settings are routine, ongoing features of every welfare state; relatively easy to manage in periods of growth, more challenging in recession and austerity.

More fundamental policy choices concern the structure of these institutions: who and what they cover, how they are funded, and how benefits are delivered. Social insurance typically covers loss of earnings due to old age, sickness, disability, and work injury. But it may not provide for extended periods of unemployment or for parental leave, and some schemes (e.g. US Medicare) provide health coverage only for the elderly and disabled. Britain's NHS covers the medical needs of the whole population free of charge but optical and dental coverage are minimal and prescription charges sometimes apply.

Access and eligibility are also important variables. Benefits may be available to all, as with America's public schools; restricted to those who have contributed, as with Social Security; or exclusively for who have served their country, as with Veterans Administration benefits. Payments may depend upon evidence of need, determined by a 'means test' that measures the applicant's resources against a subsistence standard of some kind (as with TANF), or be provided on a universal basis regardless of means (as UK child benefits and university tuition fees were until recently).

The funding of welfare programmes also varies. Social insurance is generally financed by contributions deducted from employee wages, supplemented by matching contributions from employers and government. Contributions may be flat rate or graduated; capped at a certain maximum or levied on total income. They may be gathered in an accumulating capital fund or used to pay the current generation of insurance beneficiaries. (Today, social insurance is nearly always 'pay-as-you-go'.)

Taxation is the other main funding source. (In practice, government borrowing is a third, though much less sustainable.) Taxes may be imposed by local or central governments; be progressive or regressive; and imposed on corporate or on personal earnings. They may take the form of income tax, wealth tax, consumption tax, or some combination thereof. Taxation can also be used as a redistributive instrument, with progressive income taxes, estate taxes, or capital gains taxes being used to transfer resources from rich to poor. Surprisingly, the more egalitarian welfare states of Northern Europe and Scandinavia—where marginal income taxes are comparatively high—also rely on (regressive) consumption taxes such as sales tax or Value Added Tax to a greater extent than do less generous welfare regimes such as the USA and the UK, probably because they are easier to collect than income or wealth taxes and provoke less resistance.

Welfare state programmes are government programmes. But while public authority is necessary to establish, fund, and regulate these programmes, the nature of government involvement varies. Some programmes (such as social insurance) are generally the administrative responsibility of national government; while others (such as housing, education, and personal social services) are usually administered by local authorities. In some instances, every aspect of a social programme is government-run (the US Veterans Health Administration, for example); in other systems, administrative responsibility is delegated to non-state, not-for-profit organizations.

Government agencies everywhere are increasingly outsourcing service delivery to private agencies. In the USA and the UK, social assistance and personal social services are now mostly delivered by 'purchaser-provider' arrangements of this kind. And although social work still lies at the heart of the personal social services, the professional character of social workers varies from place to place. Social workers in Germany and Sweden are civil servants or psychologically trained professionals who have discretion to tailor services to the needs of clients. In the USA, by contrast, they are often low-paid, low-status employees who act as rule-following gatekeepers and guides to a welfare system over which they exert little control.

Benefits may be paid as cash transfers, leaving the recipient free to spend them as he or she chooses, or provided 'in kind', as with public education, healthcare, or personal social services. They may also be provided as tokens (food stamps for example, or school vouchers) that may only be exchanged for a use prescribed by the programme. Social insurance benefits such as pensions, unemployment benefits, or family allowances may be the same for everyone; they may be graduated according to contributions; or they may be earnings-related, with benefits representing a particular proportion (or 'replacement rate') of the recipient's average salary. Benefit levels may even be determined by private investment decisions, as in the case of American 401(k) pension plans.

The details of a programme's coverage, access, funding, and administration determine its redistributive impact and social meaning, dictating who gets what, who pays, and how effectively the programme attracts participation. Targeted, means-tested programmes have low take-up rates and fail to reach many of the people for whom they are intended. Universal programmes are more expensive but achieve better take-up and wider support. Social perceptions and redistributive outcomes tend, in turn, to shape the political fortunes of a programme. High-quality health care and generous retirement pensions enjoy powerful cross-class support. Means-tested programmes offering low-level benefits are less popular and more vulnerable to political attack. As Richard Titmuss observed, services for the poor tend to become poor services. The most robust programmes are those that benefit the middle classes and receive solid middle-class support.

The cultural values shaping welfare state programmes also vary. Income support may be designed to enable recipients to quit the job market—providing a 'decommodified' alternative to labour market participation—or to press recipients back into work by restricting viable alternatives. Some social insurance programmes insure the male breadwinner and treat wives and children as dependants; others provide independent coverage for married women and mothers. All welfare states seek to protect children and promote 'good-enough' parenting. But conservative regimes (such as the WS1.0s of Germany, Italy, or France) provide family and child services in ways calculated to preserve traditional family structure; while Nordic nations provide amenities intended to free mothers from domestic work. All welfare states reduce reliance on charities, churches, and communities. But some minimize private welfare while others uphold the principle of 'subsidiarity', intervening only when the resources of family, church, and community have been exhausted. All welfare states seek to govern the economy, foster employment, and promote prosperity. But some are actively managerial, forging corporatist agreements, developing coordinated strategies of investment, training, and development, and deploying the macro-economic tools of demand management, while others are more restrained and indirect, relying on the effects of competition, market incentives, and monetary policy.

In short, some welfare regimes reinforce the importance of marriage; the extent of women's unpaid domestic labour; the prerogatives of employers; the importance of private charity; and the power of the market. Others do just the opposite. And each regime establishes a particular division of welfare in which the tasks of social provision are differently divided between the state, the family, and the market.

Three worlds of welfare

Real welfare states are complex systems displaying a mix of values and organizing principles. America's welfare state is predominantly liberal (or 'market-conforming') in character but the provision it makes for veterans and their families is virtually socialist and government spending on education has always been comparatively high. Sweden's social democratic regime now includes neoliberal elements and some privatized provision. And welfare states change with the result that some differences that were quite pronounced in the decades before 1980 have become less distinct in the decades since.

But despite these complexities, individual welfare states generally exhibit an overall configuration and character; if only because their disparate elements have to fit together and mesh with wider patterns of family structure, labour market, and political economy. And we can illustrate the range of possibilities by stressing the significant differences that differentiate the chief varieties of welfare regimes.

Welfare states can be differentiated by reference to size and cost. Nordic regimes are largest and most expensive, devoting as much as 30 per cent of GDP to government social expenditure; Continental regimes are intermediate, spending around 25 per cent; and Anglophone nations are smallest, with nations such as the USA spending less than 20 per cent. But spending totals are a crude measure and the numbers may be misleading. Public expenditure figures omit tax exemptions and allowances that are, in effect, welfare transfers (and are hugely important in America) and ignore the effect of taxation that 'claws back' benefits paid to high-income recipients. And large expenditures may be no indicator of generosity: unemployment expenditures increased during Mrs Thatcher's administrations, not because provision improved but because unemployment numbers massively increased.

The well-known comparative typology developed by Danish sociologist Gøsta Esping-Andersen focuses less on spending levels and more on the structuring principles that determine how welfare programmes relate to labour markets and to families. It concentrates particularly on the extent to which welfare regimes reduce the power of markets by 'decommodifying' access to goods and services (i.e. making them available as of right, outside of market exchange) and the extent to which they enhance solidarity and equalize group relations.

Using these criteria, Esping-Andersen distinguishes (i) a *social democratic* regime type, characteristic of Sweden, Norway, Denmark, and Finland, that exhibits high levels of decommodification; generous universalist benefits; strong cross-class solidarity; state rather than private provision; and a commitment to equality; (ii) a *conservative* regime, characteristic of continental European nations such as Germany, Austria, France, and Belgium, with moderate levels of decommodification; the retention of occupational hierarchies; a commitment to subsidiarity principles; and a concern to preserve traditional family structures; and (iii) a *liberal* regime, characteristic of Anglophone nations such as the USA, Canada, Australia, and New Zealand, with low levels of decommodification; low-level benefits; a preference for private forms of social provision; and an overarching concern to reinforce markets.

To give a sense of these varieties, I will describe the welfare state regimes that developed in Sweden, Germany, and the USA, each of which exemplifies a different 'world' of welfare. As we will see in later chapters, these regimes have recently begun to converge in certain respects but my concern at this point is to highlight the different forms that welfare government can take and has taken.

Sweden

Forged by a coalition of middle-class farmers and urban working classes, and developed by the Social Democratic Party under the slogan of a *Folkhemmet* ('People's Home'), Sweden's welfare state is based on cooperative economic management backed by social policies that cater to well-to-do citizens as well as those on lower incomes. Social provision is comprehensive, with universal coverage, guaranteed minimums, and basic security as a right of citizenship. Earnings-related benefits provide high replacement rates and social services are of high quality, which helps maintain middle-class support. Tax levels are high (and cash benefits are subject to 'claw-back' taxation) but Swedish citizens enjoy good state services, income security, and a relatively egalitarian society. Social services are largely state-provided, making for a strong public sector with little competition from private providers. The state is a big employer, particularly of women.

The Swedish system fosters an egalitarian, solidaristic ethos. Social insurance is 'people's insurance' that covers all citizens and, unlike conservative welfare regimes, does not distinguish between occupational groups. Redistributive taxes and transfers reduce market inequalities; rent controls and allowances make housing affordable (though in recent decades home ownership is increasingly favoured); everyone has equal access to healthcare; and good public services and benefits enable individuals to sustain a decent standard of living even when unemployed. At the same time, personal autonomy is enhanced by social arrangements that reduce the dependency of wives on husbands, children on parents, the elderly on their relatives, and employees on employers. The result is a society which combines high levels of collective provision with highly individualistic values and lifestyles.

In contrast to conservative regimes that were designed to uphold the traditional family, Swedish policies reduce the reliance of individuals on families and promote gender equality. Sweden's social policies were among the first to provide childcare, parental leave, social care for the elderly, and independent insurance for wives and mothers. Relative to GDP, Sweden spends twice as much as Germany on family services; and in the 1990s day care was guaranteed to 29 per cent of Swedish families—as against Germany's 3 per cent. (That differential has since diminished.) Women pursue higher education and enter the labour market in greater numbers than elsewhere and single mothers in particular are better supported.

Sweden's social and economic policies are tightly linked and an active labour market policy is central to the system's operation. The basic principle is the right to work (a right—and an expectation—that applies to women as well as men) but the emphasis is on the provision of training and support to enable unemployed workers to transition into jobs in growing industrial sectors rather than on continental-style employment protections that make it difficult to lay off workers. Generous insurance and social services provide security for those between jobs, encouraging flexibility and mobility. High levels of workforce participation ensure a healthy flow of payroll taxes to fund the system. And extensive social services make it easier for dual breadwinner households to raise children.

Sweden's labour market policies are part of a system of economic management in which government steers the economy in cooperation with 'the social partners'—organized business and organized labour. In contrast to liberal market regimes like the USA, where intense competition between firms and sectors is the order of the day, Swedish businesses engage in collective action vis-à-vis government and unions and benefit from the more predictable environment produced by collective agreements. These corporatist arrangements—which make labour relations more cooperative, development more planned, and capital investment more long-term—rely on a union movement that is similarly organized and capable of collective action. Sweden's large, cohesive trade unions are closely linked to the Social Democratic Party and command considerable economic and political power. (In 1996, as many as 85 per cent of the Swedish workforce was unionized; today the figure remains high at around 70 per cent.)

Swedish unions engage in economy-wide wage bargaining, forging national agreements that reduce enterprise-level conflicts and enable a measure of planning. They seek not just to maximize employment levels and union membership but also to narrow the gap between high and low pay, thereby avoiding a dualized labour market that would undermine their collective power. On occasion, they have upheld wage freezes to control inflation. And national wage agreements function not just to promote solidarity but also to shake out inefficient firms. Since wage levels are set for whole industries, efficient firms can profit and expand yet still pay average wages whereas inefficient firms are forced to improve productivity or else fold.

For much of the post-war period, Sweden has focused on promoting employment, increasing productivity, and encouraging high quality, high revenue industry. Though its governments never engaged in extensive nationalization of industry, trade, or finance, they have been especially active in assisting modernization and restructuring industry while maintaining sound fiscal policy, providing credit for industrial borrowing, supporting research and development, and investing in infrastructure, education, and training. Sweden's welfare state has succeeded in combining equity and efficiency—two goals usually seen as conflicting—achieving low levels of poverty and economic inequality, high levels of gender equality and social mobility, and high standards of living. In more recent decades, the Swedish social democratic model has faced serious challenges and governments have undertaken controversial neoliberal reforms, including the individualization of pensions and the privatization of some aspects of education, healthcare, and social services. Rising unemployment has become a problem since the 1990s and large-scale immigration has altered Swedish politics in important ways. These are issues to which we will return.

Germany

Bismarck's 19th-century social insurance laws were a conservative attempt to head off socialism and integrate key groups into the state while maintaining status and occupational hierarchies. When West Germany rebuilt its *Sozialstaat* in the aftermath of World War II, it built on that foundation, retaining its conservative character, its links to the voluntary sector, and its stratified system of occupationally distinct benefits.

The German model is like Sweden's in aiming to govern the economy through corporatist, conciliatory mechanisms and to promote social security. But unlike Sweden, it does so in ways that reproduce occupational and status differentials and reinforce traditional family structures (though in recent years these patterns have been somewhat modified). Germany provides fewer social rights and less decommodification than does Sweden, and social expenditure is smaller and less redistributive. At the same time, it imposes much more control over market processes than do the liberal states like the USA.

The German welfare state is primarily an insurance state, with a system of transfers and pensions that is notably more generous than its social services. German social insurance is overwhelmingly public in character, with private and occupational fringe benefits playing only a marginal role. Coverage is compulsory and comprehensive, and even the unemployed receive government healthcare insurance. But it is not uniform. Contributions and benefits are earnings-related and occupational status was, until quite recently, the key to benefits. The system was originally designed to sustain income and status distinctions, above all the division between blue-collar and white-collar employees. And though these differentials have become less important, groups such as the self-employed, physicians, and public servants (*Beamte*) still enjoy separate social security systems. When Germans retire, are sick, or become unemployed, their benefits reflect the salaries they enjoyed while in the workforce.

The *Sozialstaat* is also an associational state. In the 1880s, Bismarck failed in his attempted state take-over of friendly societies and voluntary insurance associations and the public-private compromise he settled for has continued ever since. Social insurance is administered by a multiplicity of occupationally distinct schemes managed by private, not-for-profit organizations run by representatives of employers and employee organizations.

These tightly regulated associations—the *Kassen*—compete to control costs and attract participants. The result is a stratified and fragmented system, especially in the field of health insurance which, as late as 1990, was administered by more than a thousand regional, occupational, and company-based plans. (Today there are many fewer *Kassen*, with just over 100 operating medical insurance, fewer still in pensions, and one single fund for unemployment.)

The *Sozialstaat* might also be described as a 'familialist' state, committed to the preservation of traditional families, though again that characteristic has been toned down in recent decades. Until quite recently German social insurance was centred on the male worker and treated wives and children as dependents. It assumed that families would take care of children and the elderly—and benefits and social services were structured accordingly. Even today, social assistance still upholds the principle of subsidiarity whereby the state is liable to provide for family needs only when the family's capacities are exhausted, and religious, charity, or community support is unavailable.

Germany has fewer women-friendly policies than Sweden and public day care was, until recently, particularly underdeveloped. (Today communes are legally obliged to supply day care.) The result is that women's labour market participation and share of total earnings are lower than in the USA and much lower than in Sweden. Ironically in view of its familialist aims—but predictably given contemporary women's desire to combine work and family—German fertility rates are comparatively low.

The 'social market economy' that Germany established in the post-war years was, like Sweden's, designed to enable an organized, corporatist approach to economic planning and development. Economy-wide collective bargaining is institutionalized, though coordination operates at the sector or industry level, rather than on a national scale. Great emphasis is placed on vocational training and human capital investment (developing specific, industry-related skills, apprenticeship schemes, and so on) and on strong employment protections. These arrangements are a boon for German manufacturing firms which have prospered in this environment, developing innovative high-quality, high-cost products that allow them to compete in international markets. On the other hand, strong job protections become more problematic during economic downturns and transitions, reducing the capacity for change and creating a gap between those in employment and the unemployed. Today, employment protections are much debated and some German companies have begun outsourcing work to self-employed subcontractors in an effort to circumvent them. Meanwhile workforce unionization has declined from 33 per cent in 1980 to 18 per cent in 2010.

The USA

The USA is the most liberal or 'market-conforming' of all the major welfare states, standing at the opposite end of the spectrum from social democratic Sweden and structured quite differently than conservative Germany. Its levels of government social expenditure are lowest, its social provision more partial, and it redistributes less than other welfare states, giving rise to some of the highest levels of poverty and inequality in the developed world. And, though 'the American Dream' suggests otherwise, intergenerational social mobility is now lower in the USA than in Sweden, Germany, or Britain.

It was not always thus. Nineteenth-century America was a leader in state welfare, providing relatively generous pensions to Civil War veterans and widows—and later to mothers and children. But the USA lacked a reformed civil service and government positions were political sinecures distributed through the party spoils system—with the result that government corruption discredited these programmes. The weakness and low prestige of the US state and the comparative strength and popularity of the private sector have been shaping influences in American welfare history ever since.

The Social Security Act of 1935 created a national system of social insurance (see Figure 7) but because of Southern resistance and

7. 'More security for the American family', *Social Security Board poster* (1939).

racial hierarchies, its coverage was far from universal. Agricultural labourers and domestic servants, most of whom were black, were not insured and the administration of social assistance (including aid to families with dependent children) was devolved to states and local authorities, many of which provided only a bare minimum.

Another legacy of America's limited (and constitutionally constrained) federal government was that the New Deal reformers chose to govern by imposing regulatory controls on private and corporate action rather than building a national infrastructure of state agencies. The result is a distinctive 'regulatory' state in which an unwieldy assortment of private actors, market mechanisms, and tax breaks is used to promote public purposes. In this context, private pensions and private health insurance took hold and became the preferred alternatives for those who could afford them. As a result, the American middle class became a powerful supporter of private sector welfare and, in alliance with employers and for-profit insurance companies, has effectively limited the development of public provision ever since.

In the 1960s, President Johnson's administration attempted to 'complete' America's welfare state with a series of 'Great Society' programmes such as Medicare (health care for seniors and the disabled), Medicaid (means-tested healthcare for the poor), federal housing subsidies, federal education funding, and food stamps. Johnson's Democratic government also passed anti-poverty legislation including the 1964 Economic Opportunity Act, Jobs Corps vocational education, and Head Start child development programmes. Within a few years, these programmes significantly reduced the number of Americans living in poverty but the 'War on Poverty' was harshly criticized by conservatives—often on thinly-disguised racial grounds—and soon discredited. Since that time, the US welfare state has continued to be incomplete, divided, and embattled.

In common with other liberal regimes, the US system is predominantly residualist, designed to supplement the market rather than displace it. It aims to secure the middle classes and alleviate extreme poverty while simultaneously supporting and reinforcing market processes. Much of its social expenditure goes to means-tested programmes and tax credits and very little to decommodification—the converse of the Swedish policy mix. And there is a decided preference for institutions such as public education that prepare people to compete in the market rather than transfer programmes that modify market outcomes: equality of opportunity, not equality of outcome is the American value.

America exhibits a predilection for the private sector and market processes: especially in healthcare (where for-profit insurance companies are prominent) and in its use of tax exemptions for private occupational benefits. This reliance on market solutions has also led successive governments to provide easy consumer credit as a substitute for welfare and as an economic stimulus, despite the risks involved in widespread private indebtedness.

Market failures such as unemployment or homelessness are addressed in ways designed to support the market rather than supplant it. There are few social or economic rights; unemployment benefits are severely time-limited; and social assistance is paid at low levels. This faith in markets and private initiative goes hand in hand with a perception of poverty as stemming from individual failure rather than from structural conditions and results in tough-minded polices that seek to change behaviour, increase work effort, limit the number of children born to single mothers, and so on.

Even among liberal regimes, America's welfare state is an outlier, lacking basic programmes that are common elsewhere. Universal healthcare, family allowances, sickness and maternity leave benefits, are standard in other developed countries but absent in the USA. (Obama's Affordable Care Act of 2010 greatly expanded healthcare coverage but as of the end of 2014 an estimated 10 per cent of Americans remained uninsured.) America provides very little public housing; public provision of family services and childcare is minimal; public transport is underdeveloped; public assistance is very patchy; and public amenities are generally limited. And though expenditure on education is comparatively high, American public schools underperform compared to those of other nations. Comparatively speaking, the public sector is disparaged and neglected.

America's welfare state is highly stratified, with sharp divisions between 'entitlements' (which are federal, contributory, rights-based, and perceived as 'deserved'); 'welfare' (which is local, non-contributory, needs-based, and 'undeserved'); and 'corporate welfare' (which consists of tax advantages and private benefits for the well to do). All of this—together with the background complexities of federalism and constitutional law—makes for a remarkably convoluted welfare state that is difficult to use, difficult to reform, and expensive to administer.

America's mode of governing the economy is also more minimal and market conforming. Serious market failures are addressed, as with the government's $700 billion bailout of the financial sector in 2008, but in normal circumstances the facilitation of free enterprise and untrammelled competition are the preferred tools for promoting growth and prosperity. The US economy exhibits few traces of the coordination and corporatism that characterize Sweden and Germany. Labour unions are weak and play little part in government. And though business lobbies buy a great deal of political influence, business leaders rarely organize on an industry-wide or economy-wide basis, preferring to compete for sectional advantage.

The US labour market is also much less regulated than in other welfare regimes. Employment protections are light; employers have hiring and firing flexibility; and there are few restraints on the distribution of income. This has given rise to a large low-wage service sector that has increased US employment levels, especially relative to conservative regimes, but has also generated a large wage dispersion, opening up a huge gap between CEO salaries and those of their average employees and creating a large class of working poor. In 2014, more than 25 per cent of the US workforce earned less than two-thirds of the national median hourly wage—a proportion of low wage workers that is the highest in the OECD. And American low wage workers are less likely than their foreign counterparts to have access to core benefits such as health insurance, sick leave, or paid vacations.

America also exhibits remarkably high levels of incarceration—running at a rate six or seven times higher than the western European average: a form of segregation and immiseration that is concentrated on the poor and minorities and which absorbs a great deal of able-bodied working age men, keeping the unemployment rate artificially low. A large proportion of social services for the poor is now distributed through correctional agencies—and jails have become the nation's largest repository for the mentally ill.

For better or for worse, Americans are more exposed to market processes than are citizens in other welfare states. The result is a highly stratified society marked by great riches, great poverty, and extreme inequality. America's welfare state reflects this pro-market, private sector bias, directing much of its spending through private channels. It is this, rather than lower overall spending levels, that distinguishes the US regime. So while American levels of gross public social expenditure are lower than the OECD average and much lower than those of Sweden or Germany, private social spending and tax-breaks given for social purposes in the USA are above average and its direct and indirect taxes are lower. The aggregate result is that America's net social spending is actually higher than the others (see Figure 8), but there are major differences in how this spending is distributed and

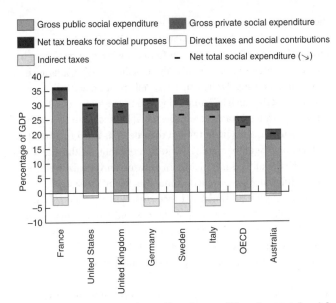

Legend:
- Gross public social expenditure
- Gross private social expenditure
- Net tax breaks for social purposes
- Direct taxes and social contributions
- Indirect taxes
- − Net total social expenditure (↘)

Percentage of GDP (y-axis: 40, 35, 30, 25, 20, 15, 10, 5, 0, −5, −10)

Countries: France, United States, United Kingdom, Germany, Sweden, Italy, OECD, Australia

8. **Public and private social spending. Gross public and net total social spending, as percentage of GDP, at market prices, 2009/10.**

the social groups that benefit. Far from being 'welfare for the poor', America's welfare state—much of which is hidden in the form of tax credits, deductions and preferences—is highly regressive, with the biggest benefits going to wealthier households.

Welfare regimes beyond the 'Three Worlds'

Esping-Andersen is a reliable guide to the most important types of welfare state existing in the western world today, even if the terrain he maps is currently changing. But there are other 'worlds of welfare' beyond the ones he describes.

Welfare states existed in Nazi Germany, Vichy France, Fascist Italy, and Peronist Argentina and played a part in the politics of nationalism, populism, and even racial eugenics that characterized these regimes. Until the 1980s, nations such as East Germany, Hungary, and Yugoslavia had 'state socialist' welfare states that provided full employment; a right to work; wide-ranging (though low-level) state services; and heavily subsidized basic goods such as food and housing. Quite generous welfare states exist today in Asian city-states such as Hong Kong and Singapore and in the Middle Eastern oil states of Saudi Arabia, United Arab Emirates, Oman, Kuwait, and Qatar, though their benefits are for nationals and do not extend to migrant workers: a reminder of the role played by the universal franchise in creating universalist welfare states. Emerging powers such China, Brazil, and India are currently developing systems of social insurance, pensions, and healthcare to cover their vast populations and provide them with a modicum of security. And the European Union increasingly coordinates the rights and protections of EU citizens living in (or moving between) its twenty-eight member states.

So the 'three worlds' typology is by no means comprehensive, being focused on the democracies of the western world and their welfare regimes as they existed in the 1980s and 1990s. Nor does every western welfare state fit neatly into one or other of its categories. Britain in particular is difficult to classify, being something of a hybrid that has changed its leading characteristics over time. A brief summary of that evolving regime will illustrate the difficulty.

In recent decades, the British welfare state has moved closer to the liberal camp where the USA and other Anglophone nations are located, but at the moment of its creation it had a much more social democratic cast. The original plan for Britain's welfare state—laid out in the celebrated Beveridge Report—envisioned an administratively streamlined, universalist system based on egalitarian principles. At its heart was the NHS—a tax-funded system offering comprehensive healthcare to everyone, free of charge. The same egalitarian universalism characterized the system of family allowances, which provided cash payments to families with children regardless of means. Universalist principles extended to National Insurance, which was based on uniform, flat-rate contributions—embodied in the stamp that each worker purchased each week—and flat-rate uniform benefits.

With its commitment to full employment and its provision of free education, free healthcare, and affordable housing, Britain's post-war welfare state promoted an encompassing sense of social citizenship. Unlike the Nordic and the continental nations, however, Britain did not develop a coordinated or corporatist style of economic management. Despite the initial nationalization of coal, steel, and the railways, governments took little direct control of industry and engaged in little economic planning—indeed Labour governments took care to appear friendly towards capital and business interests for fear of scaring away investors. Trade unions resisted corporatist agreements, preferring free collective bargaining, and employers valued free enterprise and competition over concerted action. The result was that Britain's political economy remained fundamentally liberal. Post-war governments sought to encourage investment, maintain a healthy balance of payments, and promote growth and full employment but they did so without the powerful tools of corporatist economic management. In the long run, this preference for uncoordinated, liberal capitalism would inhibit the government's ability to secure wage and price agreements, ensure industrial peace, and control inflation.

Unlike their continental competitors—most of which had to rebuild after the devastation of World War II—UK governments failed to modernize the economy and growth rates were lower than elsewhere. The result was more tightly constrained social spending, so although Britain's welfare state expanded its range, benefit levels and quality of services failed to keep pace with rising standards of living. As people became more affluent, flat rate low-level benefits ceased to offer adequate income replacement and well-to-do workers looked increasingly to the private sector. This in turn made public services appear like second rate provision for the poor, further diminishing their appeal and political viability. The NHS is an important exception, since it continues to be the basic provider of medical treatment for the whole population. But even in healthcare a private sector developed, and many now pay to avoid waiting for hip replacements or cataract operations and to stay in better appointed hospital wards. The two-tier system that emerged along with private welfare and insurance was further stratified when mass unemployment returned in the 1980s and more people came to rely on social assistance. In 1979, one in six British people relied on means-tested support: by 1997, the figure was one in three.

The UK has thus shifted from a universalistic welfare state to a more restrictive, more residualist regime that resembles the liberal US model more than it resembles the egalitarian Nordic regimes. There are, of course, still major differences separating Britain's welfare state from America's. (And just to complicate things further, Scotland's devolved welfare state institutions—higher education, social services, and NHS Scotland—are beginning to diverge from the rest of the UK.) But located on the international spectrum, these two nations now look more like each other than like their European counterparts. So when Britons or Americans discuss 'the welfare state' they should bear in mind that the versions they know best are, in important respects, among the least extensive and least generous in the western world.

Chapter 6
Problems

In ordinary conversation and political debate, a great deal of talk about the welfare state focuses on its problems. Some of this can be set aside as the complaints of ideological opponents and free-market diehards, or countered by pointing to the success of welfare states in alleviating poverty, insecurity, and ill-health. But even their most fervent proponents acknowledge that welfare states can be problem-prone and open to criticism—particularly from working people outraged by stories of 'welfare cheats', 'scroungers', and the waste of taxpayer's money. Of course many such stories are false and the public is often mistaken about the underlying facts. But not all criticism can be easily dismissed, and where supporters of the welfare state downplay its problems, critics and complaints only grow more forceful.

The welfare state is, at its core, a problem-solving apparatus, designed to manage dysfunctions that are endemic to the economic and social life of modern nations. But welfare states also generate problems of their own—moral hazards, soaring costs, labour market rigidities, bureaucratic formalism, and so on—that sometimes threaten to bring the whole enterprise into disrepute. Such problems are, as we will see, troubling and consequential. But in weighing their significance we ought always to ask: 'what can be done?' and 'what are the alternatives?' That the welfare state has its problems is undeniable. The real question is whether these problems are manageable and how they compare to those of other arrangements.

Managing not curing

Welfare state programmes are destined to be less than fully successful: it is part of their design. Markets fail and families malfunction but welfare states are not intended as *cures* for these ills: their programmes don't seek to abolish the market or replace the family with something else. If insecurity, inequality, poverty, and social exclusion continue to some extent, even within high-functioning welfare states, it is because the underlying economic and social processes that generate these outcomes remain firmly in place.

The welfare state is not an alternative to market capitalism or to the private family: it is an ameliorative adjunct to them. And it is this hybridization that explains many of the difficulties that welfare state policies encounter. As I noted earlier, welfare programmes are problem-prone because of the underlying system-conflict between the social state and market capitalism and because economic and family processes often evade regulatory controls. In contrast to command economies and totalitarian regimes, the market actors and family members addressed by welfare states are neither biddable subjects nor passive objects: they are strategic actors, inhabiting zones of private action and individual choice. Precisely because these actions have to be nudged or steered rather than commanded, a margin of non-compliance always exists.

These features ensure that welfare states are beset by difficulties. In the 1950s, the problem was the threat of inflation and limited growth. A decade later it was too much bureaucracy, too much control, and the persistence of poverty. The central problem of the 1970s was 'stagflation' (high unemployment, high inflation, and low growth); in the 1990s it was unemployment and 'dependency culture'; today it is cost containment and public debt. The system, it seems, is always in crisis. But the fact that these crises are a regular feature rather than an extraordinary one suggests they might better be understood as intrinsic characteristics of the system. And rather than foreshadowing imminent collapse, these difficulties signal the need for ongoing adjustment and reform.

Political challenges and adaptation problems

Welfare states modify market-based distributions of income, wealth, and life chances. And in doing so, they create redistributive winners and losers. The social policies of the 1950s and 1960s shifted power towards working people by empowering trade unions, compressing income inequalities, and raising standards of living for working-class families. By the same token, the neoliberal reforms of the 1980s and 1990s were not merely policy adjustments or economic adaptations. They were expressions of class and sectional interest that shifted power away from organized labour towards corporate and finance capital, weakening the public sector and empowering market forces.

Welfare reform is always a struggle over scarce resources and each new policy establishes a new front in that conflict and mobilizes a new array of interest groups. Employers and employees, retirees and young people, families with children and those without, taxpayers and welfare recipients, high earners and the low-paid each have conflicting stakes in these struggles. And because arguments over welfare intersect with conflicts over race, class, gender, and migration these disputes are often highly charged and symbolically loaded. (The tax code's hidden welfare state generally attracts much less attention.) Welfare states have always faced critics who claim that their policies are unfair or counter-productive but periodically they encounter full-scale political challenges. One such challenge—the neoliberal assault of the 1980s and 1990s—is the subject of Chapter 7.

Welfare states address problems of insecurity, poverty, ill health, and family breakup but the perceived character and preferred solutions to these problems vary across regimes and change over time. At the start of the 19th century, the age-old problem of 'the poor' became the new problem of 'the pauper'. From the 1890s onwards, that individualized conception was displaced by more structural ideas of 'poverty', 'casual labour', and 'unemployment.' By the end of the 20th century, unemployment was viewed as a supply-side problem of 'job-activation' and 're-insertion', while the problem of poverty was variously viewed as relative deprivation and social exclusion, or else as cultural pathology, inadequate work incentives, and a lack of human capital.

Ideas change over time, but so do the contexts that empower them. The welfare state operates on a socio-economic terrain that is constantly in motion. Changes in labour markets, in demographics, in household structure, in cultural values, and in citizen expectations all affect welfare state programmes and how we think about them. Because the welfare state is geared to this assemblage of moving parts, adapting to socio-economic change is an ongoing problem. The adaptation challenges that welfare states face today are the subject of Chapter 8.

Problems of administration

Political challenges and socio-economic change are processes that affect welfare states from the outside. But welfare institutions also experience problems generated by their own practices. Being a giant machine for the dispensing of cash and services, the welfare state attracts corruption and abuse that are especially irksome to the taxpaying public. As politicians love to point out, people who 'work hard and play by the rules' are incensed by the misdeeds of cheats and scroungers. And while the extent of these problems is often grossly exaggerated—welfare cheating by the poor is much less costly than tax evasion by rich—they undoubtedly occur.

Welfare cheats are a problem for any welfare system. People file false claims. They claim to be sick when they are well enough to work, or to be caring for dependants that don't exist. They receive unemployment benefits while working 'off the books' or represent themselves as seeking work when they are in fact avoiding it. Physically fit employees retire on disability benefits because colluding doctors certify them as unfit; and so on. These are genuine problems. And even if their extent is grossly overstated (see Box 8), they bring the system into disrepute.

A more serious problem, especially in welfare states where services are purchased by public agencies and delivered by private providers, is large-scale fraud by welfare providers. American newspapers report doctors who scam Medicaid; nursing home operators who overcharge the state; even juvenile court judges who are bribed to sentence youths to private detention facilities.

Of course, steps can be taken to restrict these abuses. Claims can be closely scrutinized, irregularities investigated, and violators subjected to penalties. And in most systems, this is precisely what is done. (Revealingly, more effort generally goes into investigating welfare fraud by the poor than into investigating tax fraud by the rich.) But the deeper problem is how to minimize welfare abuse while maximizing the participation and decent treatment of eligible individuals. Following the austerity policies of recent years, agencies have erred on the side of deterrence, with the

Box 8 Ronald Reagan's welfare queen story

'She used eighty names, thirty addresses, fifteen telephone numbers to collect food stamps, Social Security, veterans' benefits for four non-existing deceased veteran husbands. Her tax-free cash income alone has been running at $150,000 a year.'

Ronald Reagan, 1976. Like most 'welfare queen' stories, this one was largely mythical result that applicants are often subjected to degrading scrutiny and suspicion.

Which leads us to the problem of bad behaviour on the part of welfare agencies. Like any undertaking, welfare state agencies may be underfunded, perform poorly, provide inadequate services, behave unresponsively or condescendingly, and so on. Many of the charges levelled at welfare state programmes might therefore be better addressed to legislatures and politicians who fail to provide sufficient funding to ensure well-run agencies and quality services. Contrary to the neoliberal cliché, some problems *can* be solved by throwing money at them and the underfunding of welfare agencies is a major—and avoidable—cause of poor performance.

Agencies are often criticized for providing benefits to those not entitled, but a more common problem is the reverse: the tendency of welfare agencies to make application processes so difficult and demeaning that clients are discouraged from claiming their rightful benefits. This problem especially affects people applying for social assistance who encounter such complex and demanding procedures that applying for benefits becomes, in effect, a full-time job.

Welfare agencies can be inflexible and unresponsive. Unemployment benefits offices and job centres are often dismal, depressing places where applicants are roughly treated. Public amenities and state schools can be poorly run and underachieving. Council house tenants in Britain used to complain that local housing authorities gave them no control over their own homes, even refusing them permission to paint their front doors a colour of their choice. Overbearing bureaucracies can disempower and demoralize clients, rather than helping them develop autonomy. And welfare provision can take on an illiberal, paternalistic cast; for example in the personal social services when social work becomes moralizing social control, or in healthcare, where 'lifestyle rationing' withholds non-emergency treatment from smokers or obese patients who won't alter their unhealthy lifestyles. In today's consumer societies, people do not expect to be treated like poor law supplicants, and each time a public agency ill-treats a client, the private sector looks more attractive by comparison.

Excessive expenditures are also a problem. Public agencies are said to lack the cost-control imperatives that govern the private sector. They are, it is alleged, profligate in spending other people's money and more interested in expanding their budgets and bureaucracies than in containing costs (see Box 9). Government transfers are likened to a 'leaky bucket', with wasted funds being an inevitable part of the process.

Concerns about consumer choice, cost, and efficiency were prominent in the critical attacks of the 1980s and have since led to the restructuring and retrenchment of welfare states all around the world. The neoliberal reforms of recent decades have prioritized market mechanisms and introduced performance indicators, budget controls, and purchaser-provider arrangements as so many means of incentivizing efficiency in the public sector. But one need not embrace market fundamentalism to believe that social services ought to be efficient and enable consumer choice and client autonomy. Indeed, when progressives argue for a guaranteed minimum income and widespread decommodification, the promotion of individual autonomy forms a central part of their

Box 9 Welfare bureaucrats and 'the professional poor'

'We are fighting the big spending politicians who advocate a welfare state, the welfare bureaucrats whose jobs depend on expanding the welfare system, and the cadre of professional poor who have adopted welfare as a way of life.'

Governor Ronald Reagan, The Wall Street Journal, 1970

justification. Nor should one assume that public agencies are intrinsically less cost-effective than their private competitors: the NHS is famously efficient in its use of resources and much less expensive to run than US healthcare.

There are several ways to regulate service provision and ensure good local services. The classic WS 1.0 approach was to trust the professionals and the integrity and self-discipline of their public service ethos—and there is still much to be said for this. But regulation can also proceed by external oversight; by setting targets, budgets, and performance measures; by giving voice to clients; or by having service providers compete and allowing agencies or clients to choose between them. And benefits systems can be made simpler, more transparent, and easier to use. It is striking that Social Security is much more user-friendly than is means-tested welfare; and that single-payer healthcare (such as the NHS or Medicare) is easier to use than the highly bureaucratic private insurance system that most Americans endure.

Perverse effects

Economist Albert Hirschman has shown that conservative critics of social reform favour a trio of rhetorical tropes that he terms 'perversity', 'jeopardy', and 'futility'. Each of these is notably recurrent in the critical discourse surrounding the welfare state.

A charge especially beloved by critics is that welfare programmes backfire: that they generate unintended consequences and 'perverse' effects thereby making things worse rather than better (see Box 10). A classic instance is the case of authorities seeking to reduce the numbers of local poor by providing easily accessed benefits, only to find their generosity attracts additional claimants from elsewhere. This 'magnet effect' problem has been around a long time. In the 16th and 17th centuries, it was the problem of itinerant vagrants, masterless men, and professional beggars. Today it is the problem of 'benefit tourism' and foreign migrants

who make claims on welfare services. Instead of reducing poverty
in a locale, generous provision may serve to increase it.

One can cite many such examples—or alleged examples. Generous
benefits for the unemployed are said to reduce work effort and
create unemployment. Aid to single mothers supposedly leads
to more out-of-wedlock births. Rent controls designed to make
housing affordable allegedly reduce the supply of rental
properties. Rent subsidies enable families on benefits to live in
larger accommodation than necessary. (Britain's 'bedroom tax'
counters this by penalizing 'under-occupancy'.) Earned Income
Tax Credits may encourage employers to pay lower wages. And if
benefits are paid when a claimant's income falls below a certain
threshold, the result may be a 'poverty trap' that prevents people
from taking employment for fear of losing benefits and being
worse off.

Another version of the same problem (which economists call
'moral hazard') is the problem of companies that are 'too big to
fail'. The government's *de facto* role as an insurer of last resort and
its willingness to bail out large companies facing bankruptcy may
encourage high-risk behaviour—as the Crash of 2008 vividly

illustrated. In the opinion of some economists, the welfare state is a major source of moral hazard because it secures market actors against risk and thereby makes them less careful, less creative, and less entrepreneurial.

The claim that welfare backfires undoubtedly has powerful appeal and some basis in reality. But there is much that can be done to avoid perverse outcomes. The root cause of 'magnet' effects is geographically disparate provision, and residency requirements usually mitigate the problem. The effect can also be avoided by establishing larger administrative units and more uniform provision. The problem of able-bodied, unencumbered individuals deliberately choosing to live on benefits is generally exaggerated—though single parents may well make that choice when they otherwise lack access to childcare or healthcare—and it is much more likely if jobs are poorly paid and devoid of benefits (see Box 11). A decent minimum wage, employment benefits, and improved workplace conditions are known to reduce this effect.

Comparative and historical evidence casts doubt on the claim that generous welfare increases poverty. Sweden's benefits are comparatively generous but it has low poverty rates. US welfare for the poor is comparatively ungenerous and poverty levels are

Box 11 Welfare and the limits of choice

'As long as work pays so poorly for some women, as long as the only choice is between full-time work with little outside support and welfare, as long as the welfare system provides the only route for some women to get certain benefits such as medical care, and as long as welfare benefits can be collected independently...many people will become long-term dependants on welfare.'

Mary Bane and David Ellwood, 1994

high. Cross-national studies show poverty rates being inversely related to welfare expenditures. As for the 'too big to fail' problem, the solution is not to threaten catastrophe if risks turn bad but rather to put in place regulatory oversight ensuring that risk-taking, lending, and investments remain within secure margins.

Jeopardizing values

A second recurring complaint is that the benefits produced by welfare programmes are offset by the indirect costs that they incur. In its simplest form, this is the problem of trade-offs. Universal benefits provide transfers to those who don't need them, but have the virtue of being egalitarian and easy to administer. Targeting benefits saves money but stigmatizes recipients and reduces take-up. Earnings-related benefits attract middle-class support but reinforce inequalities. Employment protections limit corporate power and employer prerogatives—but may lead to reduced investment and labour market rigidities. Providing aid to children involves paying benefits to their parents, some of whom may be regarded as undeserving, and so on.

A more powerful challenge is the claim that welfare states jeopardize values we hold dear. This criticism accepts that welfare state programmes express important ideals but insists that they jeopardize other ideals that are equally if not more valuable: the benefits of welfare states are thus cancelled out by their hidden moral costs. Again, there are many examples. The voluntary work undertaken by families, churches, and charities may diminish because people come to regard the state as solely responsible for alleviating social problems. Providing welfare benefits may undermine autonomy, making recipients better off materially but more dependent psychologically. Long-term reliance on benefits may demoralize claimants, discouraging initiative and work effort, reducing self-respect and responsibility, and so on.

Perhaps the most familiar version of the jeopardy critique is the claim that in an effort to promote equity, welfare states undermine efficiency, thereby reducing growth and making people poorer in the long run. But despite the frequent mention of this supposed problem, empirical evidence supporting the equity–efficiency trade-off hypothesis is actually very thin, and real world cases such as Sweden indicate that it is by no means inevitable.

Welfare states may also jeopardize values indirectly by prompting changes in conduct that cumulatively undermine valued institutions. Provision of welfare benefits and services may bring about alterations in household or family structure. It may encourage divorce, single parenthood, elderly people living alone, and so on. It may weaken reciprocal obligations between family members and reduce family solidarity. In all these respects, state welfare may, it is claimed, 'undermine the family'—or at least disrupt traditional patterns of family formation and relationships.

But is this inevitable? And is it a problem? As Chapter 5 shows, until recently conservative welfare states deliberately structured benefits in ways designed to uphold the traditional family, since in these nations that family form was regarded as a good in itself. By contrast, social democratic welfare states deliberately relax the hold that families have on their members in the interest of promoting individual freedom and gender equality. One nation's tragic trade-off is, it seems, another's moral progress.

The problem of 'dependency' is similarly complex and contentious. For welfare state critics, the fact that claimants are dependent on state provision, sometimes for long periods, is a moral affront. These critics—US Senator Daniel Patrick Moynihan was famously among them—view dependency as a moral status and a psychological condition, characterized by a loss of dignity and autonomy. And this, no doubt, is a serious problem for some welfare programmes and some welfare recipients. But we should view that problem in a broader context. First of all, we should bear in mind that each of us depends on other people, relying on families, employers, or property to meet our various needs. No individual is completely autonomous—each of us relies for all sorts of support on social networks. Secondly, dependency is not an evil in itself. In welfare states with well-developed social rights, being in receipt of state benefits carries no moral stigma. And even in market-oriented regimes such as the USA or the UK, most citizens depend on the state at many points in their lives—for schooling, for healthcare, for support during transitions between jobs, for pensions, and so on. The stigma of welfare dependency is a function of political attitudes and, very often, of class and race prejudice.

A more serious problem is that long-term welfare clients may come to regard themselves as unemployable, lacking the energy and willpower—as well as the social networks and support—to help them back into work. But this too is a variable outcome and the best institutions address this problem by supporting clients without demoralizing them; helping them build capacities and develop greater autonomy.

Futility

The third recurring criticism of welfare states is that their efforts are futile and their programmes failures. This charge is especially directed at government efforts to manage the economy, to end poverty, and to reduce inequality—and comes from the Left as well as from the Right. In weighing this claim, we should bear in mind a point made earlier—that welfare states are designed to alleviate the problems of capitalist societies, not to abolish them once and for all—and that different welfare regimes prioritize different ends and succeed to varying degrees.

It is true, to take a key example, that welfare states have not ended inequality. But that can hardly count as a failure. Only social democratic regimes are explicitly egalitarian and even they don't claim to be socialist in aspiration. More problematic is the charge that welfare institutions actually *reinforce* inequality, and this does indeed occur. In conservative regimes, occupational, status, and gender inequalities are deliberately reinforced by social policy. And in liberal regimes, the wealthy and middle-class families are often the primary beneficiaries of regressive tax allowances and welfare state policies such as healthcare or higher education.

The persistence of poverty, homelessness, and untreated illness must count as more serious failures since all welfare regimes explicitly address these issues. And even if some level of failure is predictable (given the continued dominance of market processes) the extent to which these problems persist is a measure of the effectiveness of welfare regimes and their redistributive impact. The Nordics score well on these measures, as do conservative regimes such as Germany, Belgium, and the Netherlands. By contrast, the high rates of poverty in the USA and the UK are a standing affront and signal a significant failure of welfare government (see Figure 9).

The charge of futility is most often levelled at efforts to govern the economy—most vehemently by free-market critics but also by leftist thinkers who insist there is a fundamental and irreconcilable contradiction between welfare and capitalism. That latter claim would seem to have been disproved—the historical record shows that capitalism and welfare can indeed coexist and prosper together—but there are certainly failures of economic management to which one can point.

In the 1970s, the tools of Keynesian demand management (then being deployed by most western governments) failed to keep rates of unemployment and inflation within tolerable bounds, giving rise to stagflation and a prolonged period of low growth. And one frequently hears it said today that national economic management has become largely futile as a result of globalization. But this claim

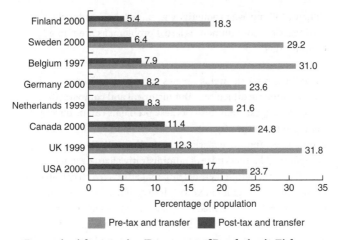

Finland 2000	5.4	18.3
Sweden 2000	6.4	29.2
Belgium 1997	7.9	31.0
Germany 2000	8.2	23.6
Netherlands 1999	8.3	21.6
Canada 2000	11.4	24.8
UK 1999	12.3	31.8
USA 2000	17	23.7

Percentage of population

■ Pre-tax and transfer   ■ Post-tax and transfer

**9. Poverty in eight countries. 'Percentages of Population in Eight
Countries with Disposable Incomes Less than 1/2 the National
Median'.**

too, is overstated. It is true that national borders are more porous
and the governing capacities of nation-states have diminished.
But they have by no means declined to zero, and certain
governments—again the Nordics do best—have been very effective
in maintaining macroeconomic stability and growth. At the same
time, there have undoubtedly been instances—Greece in 2015
is a case in point—where national governments have failed to
implement sustainable fiscal policies or secure a reliable tax
base with the result that their welfare states have come close
to collapse.

Even when welfare institutions function well they often fall
victim to their own success, giving rise to new needs, heightened
expectations, and increased costs. In healthcare, for example,
costs increase as sophisticated technologies and treatments
become available and as patients come to expect improved levels
of provision. Education costs move in the same direction, as do
the costs of personal social services, not least because it is

difficult to improve productivity in these labour-intensive settings. Cost containment is a real problem, as are rising expectations.

In all these respects, welfare states encounter serious, sometimes insurmountable difficulties. But historical and comparative evidence suggests that most of these problems can be effectively managed given the requisite political will and administrative competence. Indeed, experience of dealing with these challenges has generated a repertoire of administrative fixes designed to curtail and moderate their detrimental effects. Poverty traps can be diminished by graduated withdrawal of benefits; income support can be conditioned on evidence of job-seeking or care-giving responsibilities; insurance contributions and benefits can be brought into balanced alignment; unemployment benefits can be linked to labour market activation schemes; wealthy individuals and corporations can be made to pay a greater share of tax, and so on.

The welfare state's opponents despair of these problems and present them as fatal flaws. But in the real world of administration, problems are mostly amenable to pragmatic solutions of one kind or another. Moreover, many of these 'welfare problems' can be directly traced to underlying market failures—labour markets that don't clear, uninsurable risks, imperfect information, imperfect competition, and so on. To regard them as the welfare state's fatal flaws is to express a political animus that is not grounded in administrative experience.

The welfare state often seems bedevilled by problems. And that, indeed, is how its critics and opponents like to characterize it. But we ought to view these problems in the context of the welfare state's structural functions and the system-conflicts they entail. We need to recall that welfare states operate in conflictual combination with market economies and that it is this contradiction that generates many of the problems. We might also observe that the most problematic welfare states are not the largest, most expansive ones, but rather those in liberal regimes, where weak welfare state mechanisms are poorly integrated with powerful market economies.

Chapter 7
Neoliberalism and WS 2.0

The welfare states that enjoyed three decades of expansion after 1945 have endured a challenging period in the decades since. Beginning in the late 1970s, in one country after another, opposition groups mounted a sustained attack on welfare states in the name of free markets and conservative family values. More recently, political leaders and policymakers have struggled to adapt welfare state programmes to meet the challenges of the post-industrial world in which they nowadays operate. Both these developments—the neoliberal assault and the post-industrial adaptations—are, in their different ways, responses to socio-economic transformations driven by late 20th-century capitalism: changes that were initially experienced as an economic crisis and later as a shift in prevailing modes of production and social organization. This chapter describes the first of these phases: the economic crisis of the 1970s and the neoliberal onslaught it unleashed. Chapter 8 discusses the socio-economic transformations and adaptive reforms that are currently unfolding.

The 'New Right' coalition

Amidst the economic disruptions of the 1970s, a coalition of free-market and socially conservative political forces seized the opportunity to push back against the post-war welfare state and the balances of power it established. The loudest voices in this 'New Right' movement demanded the abolition of the welfare state and a return to free markets, self-help, and private charity. But though this radical approach often set the terms of debate, the movement's political leaders were more pragmatic, targeting unpopular aspects of the welfare system, such as social assistance for the poor, rather than broadly-supported middle-class programmes such as Social Security or the NHS.

Despite their political dominance in the 1980s and 1990s, New Right reformers did not in the end abolish the welfare state—not even in the USA where welfare state government has always been most embattled. Indeed the failure of their prolonged assault might be taken as proof of the impossibility of doing without a welfare state, at least where democratic processes still operate. But even as they fell short of their goals, reformers succeeded in changing the character of welfare states, creating a less expansive, more austere version—let's call it 'WS 2.0'—based on a neoliberal, 'de-regulating' style of economic government and a market-oriented reworking of social policy.

The impact of the neoliberal challenge has been felt in welfare states everywhere. Germany reformed its labour market policies, reduced unemployment benefits, and curtailed federal spending. Sweden cut taxes, partly privatized social security, and tolerated unprecedented levels of unemployment. But the heartland of neoliberal reform was in the liberal Anglophone nations: in Canada, Australia, New Zealand, and above all, America and Britain. And it is on these last two nations that my discussion will concentrate.

Economic downturn

In the mid-1970s a steep and prolonged economic downturn began, affecting welfare states everywhere. Expanding markets, cheap energy, and stable money had enabled post-war growth and welfare state expansion but from the late 1960s onwards, falling rates of profit, declining productivity, balance of payments problems, budget deficits, and recurring fiscal crises signalled that the world economy was slowing down and welfare states appeared to be reaching the limits of growth.

It was the OPEC oil shock of 1973 that precipitated the crisis but equally important was the prior collapse of Bretton Woods—a framework of international monetary controls that had enabled national governments to manage their economies and allowed welfare states to flourish. Without the discipline of the system's fixed exchange rates, governments spent more and fuelled inflation, causing instability in the currency markets. When, as a result, investment fell and unemployment rose, government efforts to stimulate demand set off an inflationary spiral. US inflation rates topped 10 per cent in the mid-1970s, peaking at 13.5 per cent by the end of the decade. UK rates rose even higher, reaching 24 per cent in 1975. Against this troubled background, OPEC's decision to end cheap energy threw western economies into turmoil. Within months, the price of oil doubled, stock markets plunged, inflation surged, and unemployment began its steep upward climb.

Industrial relations entered a new era of instability—a militant period of strikes, stoppages, and demonstrations that shook public faith in the capacity of western governments to govern. Distributional conflicts that had been effectively managed in the growth decades (when rising productivity enabled wage increases and rising incomes enabled higher taxes) now became sharper and more divisive. Welfare state funding came under pressure as rising unemployment reduced tax receipts and insurance contributions while increasing benefit payments. Efforts to fill the fiscal hole by increasing taxes met with stiff resistance.

Political response

Western governments at first reacted by applying the standard Keynesian formulas: increasing expenditure and lowering interest rates to buoy up aggregate demand and encourage job creation. But the familiar recipes were no longer working. Instead of reducing unemployment, increased spending heightened inflation, resulting in the toxic coexistence of recession and inflation—an anomaly that cast doubt on the conceptual basis of post-war economic management and left governments uncertain as to how to proceed.

Under pressure from international markets, governments decided they had little choice but to abandon expansionist policies and focus instead on cutting public expenditure and establishing 'sound money'. In a historic reversal of priorities, control of inflation replaced full employment as the primary economic objective—with devastating effects on the numbers of people out of work. Ironically, it was the Democratic and Labour governments of President Carter and Prime Minister Callaghan (see Box 12) that first undertook this political *volte-face*. But these efforts only succeeded in reducing their electoral support and reinforcing the view that serious reform could best be undertaken by right-wing parties less closely associated with trade unions and with the tax-and-spend policies of the welfare state.

Conservative politicians seized their opportunity. Margaret Thatcher and Ronald Reagan led the way, each of them assailing the post-war settlement with powerful rhetorical attacks combining neoliberal economic prescriptions with neoconservative nostrums designed to reassert national 'greatness' and reverse the cultural changes of the 1960s. Blame for their

Box 12 The crisis of Keynesianism

'We used to think you could just spend your way out of a recession and increase employment by cutting taxes and boosting spending. I tell you in all candour that option no longer exists.'

Prime Minister James Callaghan, addressing the Labour Party Conference, 1976

nations' economic and moral decline lay, they insisted, at the door of labour unions, left-of-centre politics, and the welfare state. The solution was to curtail the power of organized labour; reduce social expenditure; raise interest rates; cut taxes; and embrace open markets. They also sought to transform the state, building its military strength while reducing its role in social and economic affairs. If the classic liberal state was a minimalist one, the New Right state was to be minimal in some respects but strong in others. 'Big government' was a beast to be starved—preferably by cutting taxes—and the public sector was to be reduced to a minimum. (As anti-tax crusader Grover Norquist put it: 'Our goal is to shrink government to the size where we can drown it in the bathtub.') But at the same time a powerful state was needed: to maintain national strength abroad; force through economic reforms; cut public spending programmes and taxes; privatize public assets; abolish regulatory controls—and deal with the resistance that these reforms generated (see Figure 10).

In all of this, politicians drew upon the ideas of libertarian intellectuals and free-market economists such as Friedrich Hayek

10. **Striking miners and police during the 1984–5 British miners' strike, Bilsten Glen Colliery, Scotland.**

and Milton Friedman as well as the practical support of the right-wing 'think tanks' that emerged in this period, generously supported by the business community. Soon neoliberalism was shaping the policies of other western governments, being embraced by centre-left parties, and dominating international institutions such as the IMF, the World Bank, the OECD, and the EU. By the 1990s, the post-war welfare state settlement was being replaced by a new 'Washington Consensus' that pressed for globalization, free trade, free flows of capital, and deregulated labour markets.

Neoliberal government

From the 1980s onwards, US and UK governments abandoned their commitment to full employment and Keynesian demand management in favour first of 'monetarism', which prioritized inflation control and 'sound money' and then 'supply-side' policies, which sought to reawaken enterprise and restore incentives by cutting social spending and taxation. The predictable result was a massive rise in unemployment. Around 1.5 million Britons were out of work when Mrs Thatcher was elected in 1979 (a rate of 5.4 per cent); by the end of her first term that number had more than doubled to over 3 million (11.9 per cent). In the early 1980s, the US unemployment rate rose to nearly 10 per cent: twice the rate of previous decades.

Mass unemployment helped right-of-centre governments undermine the power of the unions, force through wage cuts and flexibility agreements, and de-regulate labour markets by relaxing restrictions on hiring, layoffs, and wages. In America and Britain, industries such as coal, steel, shipbuilding, and car manufacture—all heavily unionized—were allowed to collapse even as governments elsewhere (in Germany and Sweden for instance) invested in the modernization of these sectors in the belief that they were vital to the nation's economic health. The numbers employed in manufacturing plummeted, along with union membership.

The new pro-market policies divided working people, separating those in well-paid, secure jobs from the unemployed and those in precarious employment. The Conservative and Republican parties assiduously courted disaffected Labour and Democratic voters, targeting a demographic of affluent workers who owned their homes and preferred tax cuts to welfare benefits. In this changed electoral landscape, market-friendly policies favouring the better off ceased to be off-limits and were seen instead as essential to encourage enterprise and improve international competitiveness. Tax cuts and benefits for the rich would, it was claimed, eventually 'trickle down' to benefit everyone.

The neoliberal reforms of the 1980s and 1990s reversed the social and economic orthodoxies of the post-war decades. Tax cuts were everywhere emphasized, even as the poor had their benefits cut and despite the large deficits they produced. Nationalized firms, public utilities, and public assets were sold off to raise revenues and transfer control from public to private hands. In the short term, privatizations provided windfalls for hard-pressed Treasury departments coping with higher unemployment and reduced tax revenues. In the longer run, they shrank the size of the public sector and with it, the power of public sector unions. Where the sell-offs were popular with the electorate—as with council house sales (which greatly reduced Britain's stock of social housing) or British Telecom's 1984 huge public share issue—they expanded the extent of homeownership and shareholding and enlarged the appeal of conservative parties.

The deregulation of banking and finance was another major policy change. From the 1980s onwards, banks lost their monopoly over lending and large retail firms provided financial services to customers, creating a financialized economy in which profits flowed primarily from credit and financing rather than from manufacture. One result was a massive expansion of consumer credit, making it easier for households to borrow, even in the absence of substantial assets or secure incomes. Easy credit

11. Average number of capital controls for fifteen OECD countries.

operated as a substitute for wage rises and improved welfare benefits, swelling aggregate demand and ushering in the boom years of the 1990s. It was, as sociologist Colin Crouch observed, 'privatized Keynesianism'.

Deregulation extended to the currency and capital markets, which were now 'liberalized' from the restrictions of the Bretton Woods era (see Figure 11). Exchange controls were abolished, unleashing the flow of trade, finance, currency, and capital.

The results, as usual, were mixed, with massive gains going to the financial centres of London and New York but at a cost of increased exposure of domestic industry to international competition.

Attacking the welfare state

Libertarians had long regarded the welfare state as an abomination that undermined the operation of markets and the freedom of individuals. Conservative classics like Hilaire Belloc's 'The Servile State' and Hayek's 'The Road to Serfdom' portrayed it as a path to totalitarianism—a view that found echoes in the writings of Milton Friedman and Chicago School economists. For most of the 20th century, these beliefs had few mainstream adherents but in the crisis-ridden context of the 1970s, they gained influence, feeding into anxieties about social and cultural change as well as widespread economic frustration.

For many on the Right, the welfare state was fundamentally misconceived: getting in the way of enterprise and industry, undermining the market economy, and demoralizing those it claimed to help. This critique was especially powerful in liberal regimes where welfare institutions were residual and where many labour-intensive and service sector firms competed on cost rather than quality. Policy challenges that might have been viewed as problems of adaptation or maladministration were presented as insurmountable difficulties. Negative political interpretations were projected onto any and every problem, making each new difficulty another reason to abandon the welfare state. And of course the standard critiques—welfare produces perverse effects; welfare jeopardizes cherished values; welfare is futile—were rolled out, dusted off, and applied to every instance of welfare state government.

Welfare states were blamed for ending growth and fostering the economic downturn. Instead of permitting benign market forces to work unhindered, maximizing competition and efficiency, the welfare state interfered with the market's self-regulating order, allowing 'special interests' (unions and public employees) to distort market signals and introduce 'rigidities' (employment rights) into labour markets that ought to be fluid and flexible. That welfare states had come into existence precisely because free markets produce calamitous effects; that welfare states had enabled a prolonged period of unprecedented growth; that cross-national evidence refuted the claim that welfare states were a drag on economic performance, and that big corporations were the major 'special interests' shaping government policy—these were considerations that got lost in the clamorous rush to discredit welfare state government.

Welfare reform

The assault on welfare states began with a battle for hearts and minds. Reform proposals were accompanied by a steady drumbeat of criticism, in which welfare states were demeaned and demonized. The welfare state was a socialist monstrosity sapping the nation's spirit and ruining its economy. The public sector was costly, bureaucratic, and inefficient. Welfare clients were cheats and scroungers. Handouts were the opium of the masses, leading to dependency, idleness, drugs, and crime (see Box 13).

The first reforms—beyond the endless 'efficiency reviews' that governments began to put in place—were simple cutbacks: reductions in benefits, reductions in the scope and quality of social services, a tightening of eligibility conditions. Cost-cutting ministers looked at every head of expenditure but political prudence ensured that cuts mostly targeted discretionary social assistance programmes rather than pensions or healthcare.

Reformers sought to eradicate any trace of 'dependency culture' that might discourage benefit recipients from finding work, forming marriages, or cultivating personal independence. This attack on dependency—which drew on the writings of academics

Box 13 The evils of social provision

'Welfare benefits, distributed with little or no consideration of their effects on behaviour, encouraged illegitimacy, facilitated the breakdown of families, and replaced incentives favouring work and self-reliance with perverse encouragement for idleness and cheating.'

Margaret Thatcher, 1993

such as Lawrence Mead and Charles Murray and became something of an obsession among social conservatives—began by imposing new behavioural requirements and making benefits more conditional. Instead of being a right or entitlement, income support was made conditional on changes in the recipient's conduct. Those receiving social assistance—above all single parents and the long-term unemployed—were required to demonstrate that they were actively seeking work, engaging in job training, or obtaining educational qualifications. And government spending increasingly favoured tax credits for the working poor rather than assistance for out-of-work individuals, leaving those in extreme poverty to turn to food banks, relatives, and survival strategies of one kind or another.

In Britain, unemployment benefits became 'Jobseeker's Allowances' and a new emphasis was placed on 'welfare to work'—though these efforts ran up against the shortage of real jobs and the limits of government job-creation schemes. In the US, President Clinton signed the Personal Responsibility and Work Opportunity Reconciliation Act (1996)—abolishing the federal programme providing aid to dependent children and their parents and replacing it with a more restrictive, state-run scheme entitled Temporary Assistance to Needy Families. TANF required single mothers to find work if they wanted to receive welfare benefits—thereby reversing the original purpose of such aid, which had been to enable widows and single mothers to stay home to care for their children.

Encouraging a return to work and helping individuals avoid long-term reliance on welfare are ideas with widespread support: social democratic welfare regimes have long adopted the same principles. But in America and Britain—in a context of mass unemployment, low-wage labour markets, and with an absence of supporting institutions such as free public childcare—these policies took a much harsher form. As sociologist Jamie Peck remarked, 'Workfare is not about creating jobs for people that don't have them; it is about creating workers for jobs that nobody wants.'

Cutbacks also affected public sector jobs, particularly in the USA where reducing the size of the federal government became an aim of successive Republican administrations. President George W. Bush shrank the federal government to a point where it was, in relative terms, smaller than at any point since 1940—a job destruction programme that disproportionately affected minorities and further reduced the capacities and competence of the American state.

Neoliberal management

Governments tightened welfare funding and cut back benefits but these were policy adjustments that might later be reversed when prosperity returned. (And in fact the New Labour governments of Tony Blair and Gordon Brown did just that in many areas.) A more radical, and more enduring programme of structural reform has changed how welfare agencies are funded and managed, and the ways in which benefits and services are delivered.

Neoliberals had long insisted that goods such as housing, health, education, and pensions could be more efficiently supplied by the market than by the state. Given the impossibility of abolishing the welfare state and returning to unregulated markets, their preferred solution was to restructure welfare institutions in ways that made them behave more like market actors. To this end, a series of managerial reforms—the 'new public management'—was introduced, applying to public agencies a number of private sector techniques such as cash-limits, target setting, and performance-indicators. Subsequently, internal markets and competitive practices were introduced to break up the 'monopolies' enjoyed by public housing, hospitals, schools, and universities, and induce these institutions to function more cost-effectively.

Another neoliberal reform was the establishment of 'contracting out' and 'purchaser-provider' arrangements. This restructuring ended the old system whereby public agencies received funding, delivered services, and monitored their own performance, replacing it with a more complex, marketized arrangement in which public agencies are required to contract out the task of delivering services to private firms that compete to get the work. The new system—which relies on competitive tendering to drive down costs and improve service quality—has effectively privatized much social care.

Vouchers and 'opt-outs' had similar effects. Instead of financing housing or education authorities, public funding (in the form of vouchers) goes directly to 'consumers' who are allowed to choose which schools or housing they will 'buy' into. And opt-out schemes permit individuals to quit public sector schemes and 'go private': for example, leaving the public pension scheme and insuring oneself in the commercial market. Although it is frequently proposed, the privatization of National Insurance and Social Security has proven politically unfeasible, and neoliberal reformers have had to settle for a system in which individuals are incentivized to supplement publicly insured pensions and healthcare with personal policies purchased in the private sector.

Neoliberalism's impact

Neoliberal policies were, no doubt, intended to generate prosperity and enhance welfare. And economies run on neoliberal principles sometimes do prosper, as the USA and the UK showed in the boom years of the 1990s and early 2000s. But as well as being destabilizing (as the 2008 crisis showed) neoliberal policies are profoundly inegalitarian and heavily biased towards powerful market actors. Their immediate, direct benefits go to the rich not the poor; to employers not employees; to capital not to labour. And they are party-political in their impact, tending to reduce support for the parties of the welfare state and increase it for parties aligned with business and markets.

WS 1.0 generally advanced the interests of industrial workers, creating a prosperous middle class, and increasing living standards for the vast majority of families. Its expansion was accompanied by a large-scale shift in income distribution, narrowing the gap between top and bottom earners, creating more equal societies in which fewer people were either very poor or very rich. The policies of the 1980s and 1990s reversed these developments. For the most part, they worked to the advantage of corporate executives, finance capitalists, large employers, and property-owners. They restored the power of economic elites, re-established conditions for capital accumulation, and shifted power and influence towards finance capital. In the course of a few decades, they undid the equalizing, democratizing effects that the New Deal and the welfare state had achieved (see Figure 12).

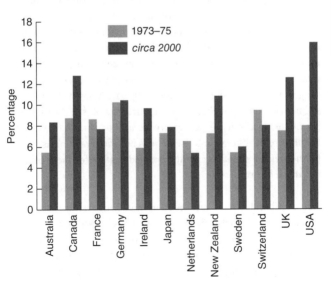

12. Income share (excluding capital gains) of the top 1 per cent in affluent democracies.

The weakening of economic and social rights reinforced these new inequalities. Governments in America, Britain, and elsewhere took steps to make labour markets more flexible, which generally meant more precarious for workers. Employment protections were weakened; the union movement collapsed; wage stagnation continued despite longer hours and improved productivity; new industrial relations laws favoured employers; tax rates were reduced and funding for discretionary social spending was withdrawn. The result is a 'winner takes all' economy, in which the rich are rewarded, the poor are pressurized, and those in the middle are rendered more insecure.

But despite these radical transformations, despite the falling off in social assistance, and despite the emphasis on choice, consumerism, and competition that is the hallmark of WS 2.0, it is a striking fact that the core institutions of the original welfare state have largely survived and remain firmly in place today. The welfare state's corporate and plutocratic opponents have regained their economic and political ascendancy but they have left its middle-class institutions more or less untouched. Indeed, the international evidence shows that the major welfare state programmes of pensions (see Figure 13), unemployment and sickness benefits (see Figure 14), and healthcare (see Figure 15) provide more extensive, generous coverage today than they did at the start of neoliberalism's rise to power. Neoliberalism's assault on the welfare state has chiefly impacted welfare for those in need; not those in work.

The neoliberal assault succeeded in modifying welfare states everywhere, restructuring the programmes of WS 1.0 into the more market-oriented forms of WS 2.0 and bringing to an end the remarkable expansion of the post-war decades. But after thirty years of political dominance, neoliberalism has neither displaced nor dismantled the fundamental institutions of welfare state government nor has it diminished their continuing

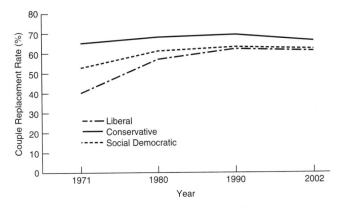

13. Standard pension benefit, 1971–2002, in social democratic, conservative, and liberal regimes.

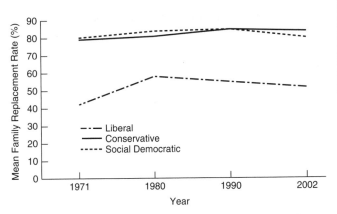

14. Sickness benefit, 1971–2002, in social democratic, conservative, and liberal regimes.

popularity with the electorate. Instead, taxes and social expenditures as a share of GDP have levelled off—at different rates in different regimes—and reforms have mostly assumed steady-state funding rather than the rapid growth of the earlier period. This does not mean, of course, that such dismantling

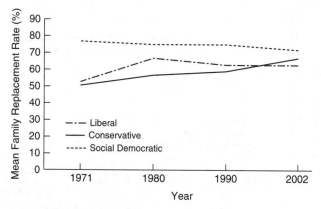

15. Unemployment benefit, 1971–2002, in social democratic, conservative, and liberal regimes.

may not occur in the future in one nation or another. But it does mean that welfare states have shown themselves to be remarkably durable and resilient in the face of very powerful opposition.

Chapter 8
Post-industrial transitions: towards WS 3.0

If they are to remain vital and effective, welfare states must adapt to changing circumstances. Social and economic processes are constantly in motion, so the adjustment and updating of policy is an integral, ongoing part of welfare government. (Indeed, where programmes are not indexed-linked, changes in living costs or in patterns of compensation affect the value of benefits, tax credits, and allowances making inaction a significant policy choice.) But social and economic change sometimes takes a deeper, more structural form and necessitates policy change of a more fundamental nature. Today, in all the western nations, a paradigm change of this kind is underway.

For several decades now, the world's advanced nations have been transitioning from industrial to post-industrial production—an economic transformation accompanied by wide-ranging changes in social, political, and cultural relations. Welfare states have increasingly had to deal with new kinds of social risk and new forms of economic insecurity as well as new difficulties dealing with the older problems for which they were designed. Adjusting to these upheavals is a challenge for welfare state governance everywhere. And although national responses vary, the evidence suggests that a common set of solutions is currently being developed: a new generation of policies that we might prospectively call 'Welfare State 3.0'.

When the disruptive effects of these transformations first made themselves felt in the 1970s, welfare state opponents seized the opportunity to press a radical, free-market agenda, representing the problems associated with structural transition as proof that welfare state government was no longer viable. And although some of the reforms they introduced have been widely embraced—improved accountability for public agencies, for example, or enhanced choice for service users—neoliberals were more concerned to reduce welfare state government than to adapt it to new times. But the heyday of neoliberalism now appears to be passing, even in its US and UK heartlands, and government policymakers are increasingly focusing on the challenge of making welfare states fit for a post-industrial world.

WS 1.0 emerged within a specific historical conjuncture and was designed to fit a particular set of social and economic circumstances. While these circumstances continued, the welfare state was viewed as a remarkable success story, fostering broadly shared economic prosperity, creating relatively affluent middle classes, and raising the living standards of the worst-off citizens. But times have changed and the need for adaption and renewal is now a major policy challenge and a political problem for welfare states everywhere.

A changing world economy

Sustained economic growth and welfare state expansion were made possible in the post-war decades by an expanding world economy, the dominance of western manufacturing, cheap energy, a stable international monetary system, and a Fordist regime of mass production and mass consumption. They were also enabled by the framework of commercial and financial relations set up at Bretton Woods in 1944—a set of institutions that facilitated trade, funded development, and maintained fixed exchange rates while providing national economies with a measure of control over their own fates. Under this system of 'embedded liberalism', individual states could limit the cross-border movement of capital and currency, thereby protecting their economies from the full force of international competition. And because domestic investors, producers, and consumers had few exit options, it allowed governments to regulate labour markets and fund social spending.

Bretton Woods survived until 1971 when the US government, hard pressed by the costs of Vietnam (an unpopular war that was waged without tax raises to fund it), a large trade deficit, and recurring runs on its currency, unilaterally devalued the dollar and ended its convertibility into gold—a development that destabilized the international system and relaxed the controls that had disciplined national economies. At the same time, the expansionist phase of world economic development came to an end and a period of contraction began, marked by severe recessions, low economic growth, and high rates of unemployment—all of which adversely affected welfare state funding. When the OPEC nations doubled the price of oil in 1973, effectively ending the era of cheap energy, it plunged western economies into deep recession.

Globalization

Globalization—the integration of economic and social relations on a world scale—is driven by technological advance: by ultra-rapid transport, containerization, electronic communications, super-computers, and so on. But it is also propelled by the cross-border reach of multinational corporations, by regional trade agreements and economic integration, and by the political choices of nation-states. From the late 1970s onwards, these transnational phenomena increased in importance as governments opened their economies to international markets, removing tariffs, relaxing restrictions, and enabling free flows of capital, currency, and labour.

Post-war welfare states developed in a world where national governments could set the terms for economic action within their borders. Increased internationalization of trade, production, and consumption, together with the deregulation of financial, capital, and currency markets, have made that much less possible. Instead of being accountable solely to their electorates, governments must now seek the approval of international markets which stand ready to punish profligate social spending, high corporate tax rates, or above-average inflation. Meanwhile, EU member states are increasingly pressed to coordinate social protections and labour market policies within the constraints imposed by monetary union. The economic autonomy of individual states is thereby diminished, as is their room for manoeuvre in setting social policies.

De-industrialization

In post-war western economies the leading industries were Fordist assembly line manufacturers, employing large numbers of semi-skilled male workers to mass produce consumer durables for domestic markets. These manufacturing sectors powered economic growth, increasing productivity through economies of scale and technological advance, raising consumer demand with steadily rising wages, and increasing profits as markets expanded. The result was a sustained period of full employment, providing low-skilled male workers with secure, unionized jobs, improved workplace conditions, and an expanded range of welfare services.

By the mid-1970s, this too began to change. Manufacturing jobs moved to low-wage economies in developing nations, taking advantage of reduced transportation costs and the new freedom to invest abroad. In the industries that remained, advanced production techniques reduced the numbers of workers and placed a premium on highly skilled employees. In 1960, 35 per cent of the US workforce had industrial jobs: today less than 20 per cent do. Over the same period, the UK has seen manufacturing sector jobs fall by half.

De-industrialization—and a shift to a more service-based economy—has occurred in all the OECD countries, though its timing, extent, and consequences vary. Nations such as Germany and Sweden have taken steps to retain a modernized industrial sector focused on high-skilled, quality production. But the larger western pattern is the decline of manufacturing industry and the rise of a more skill-differentiated service sector, with major consequences for the nature of employment.

Labour markets

WS 1.0 was premised on certain labour market assumptions. Its planners assumed full employment in manufacturing and agriculture, with male workers earning a family wage sufficient to provide for dependants, a prospect of life-long employment, and steadily increasing wages. Seventy years later, few of these assumptions hold good. From the 1970s onwards, western countries experienced large rises in unemployment, the real income of working people stagnated, and an increasingly precarious labour market generated large numbers of long-term unemployed, underemployed, and 'working poor.' People with jobs now work more intensively for longer hours and 'dual earner' households have replaced the breadwinner-and-housewife model of the 1950s. Work is unevenly distributed, with divisions between work-rich and work-poor households, and large groups of 'supernumeraries' that labour markets fail to absorb—young people in search of a first job, ageing workers made redundant, people who have never worked. Prior to 1970, low-skilled workers could find steady, unionized jobs in industries where technological advances resulted in improved productivity and rising wages. Today, the low-skilled are often jobless or employed in service jobs with little scope for improved productivity and few employment protections.

De-industrialization has increased unemployment, altered gender patterns, and changed the skills that are in demand. Average unemployment levels in the UK went from one-third of a million in the 1950s, to half a million in the 1960s, to nearly one million in the 1970s and more than two and a half million throughout the 1980s. An economy dominated by manufacturing and blue-collar jobs shifted to one characterized by services and white-collar jobs while the gender composition of the workforce changed from two-thirds male to one-half female.

The decline of industrial production has meant that unskilled and semi-skilled unionized jobs for men have become increasingly scarce (see Figure 16). And though service industries have taken up some of the slack, the low-skilled jobs generated by services such as retail, cleaning, catering, security, and social care are less well paid, often part-time or temporary, rarely unionized, and filled by women rather than men. The result is that male manual workers have become jobless while married working-class women have entered the workforce in ever-greater numbers. In high-tech services such as finance, IT, business, and healthcare there is a premium on higher education, technical skills, and scientific

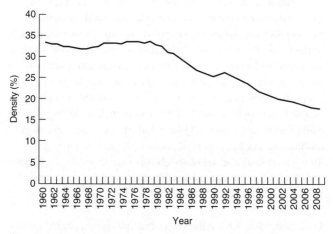

16. **Union density, OECD, 1960–2008.**

training—and employees in these sectors command high salaries and fringe benefits. (Though privately-provided pension plans are becoming less common and less generous—shifting from defined benefit to defined contribution—thereby making even affluent employees somewhat less secure.) At the lower end of the market, employment is increasingly precarious and poorly paid with large numbers of workers in casual employment, with 'on-call schedules' and 'zero hours' contracts.

Nations vary, of course, as do policy responses to economic trends and market forces. Governments in the USA and the UK have reduced union power, deregulated labour markets, and enabled employers to pay poverty wages. The regimes of continental Europe and Scandinavia have mostly maintained trade unions as social partners, upheld minimum wages, and retained employment protections. But every economy has been subject to structural upheaval and governments have had to choose between higher levels of unemployment or larger numbers of working poor.

Gender and family

Post-war welfare states were designed to secure male breadwinners on the assumption that their 'family wage' would meet the needs of wives and children. And they took for granted the existence of stable families where women provided domestic labour and cared for children and elderly relatives. The unpaid welfare services supplied by housewives, mothers, and daughters were an essential supplement to state welfare and effectively subsidized WS 1.0.

Today, as more women move into paid work, as fewer men's wages can support a family, as more marriages end in divorce or separation, and as more people set up home alone or as single parents, that supply of unpaid welfare is greatly diminished. Again, these trends have serious consequences for welfare states, especially in Nordic and liberal welfare regimes where divorce and out-of-wedlock birth rates are high. (More than half of all children in Scandinavia and the USA grow up without both biological parents.)

Of course the primary effect of women's entry into the labour market—together with liberalized divorce laws, benefits for single parents, and enhanced social services—has been to reduce women's dependence on men and increase their control over their own lives and careers. But with new freedoms come new risks, and these developments have created challenges for welfare states struggling to deal with the fall-out of family break-up, the needs of working mothers, and the problems of an increasingly diverse set of households.

Demography

Population characteristics and dynamics are of the utmost importance for welfare states. In the 1950s and 1960s, western nations had small numbers of elderly and large numbers of working-age people, making for a healthy 'dependency rate'—i.e. a favourable ratio of many contributing workers to few welfare state beneficiaries. In subsequent decades, these actuarial advantages disappeared. People lived longer and the elderly population expanded, as did the numbers of very aged people. When Old Age Pensions were introduced in Britain in 1907, life expectancy was 48 years for men and 49 for women. Few people lived long enough to claim the pension to which they were entitled at age 70. Today's life expectancies are 75 and 80 years respectively and the population of retirees drawing pensions—eligibility for which started, until very recently, at 65 for men and 60 for women—has grown dramatically. In 2009, 13 per cent of America's population was aged 65 or older; in the UK, the figure was 16 per cent with that population group projected to double over the next 35 years.

The extension of the life course is a tremendous boon, particularly where the elderly remain healthy and enjoy sufficient resources.

And it is surely one of the welfare state's greatest accomplishments to have enabled older people to retire from work and live in relative security and comfort. But an ageing population brings increased costs and imposes heavy burdens on health and social services as well as on state pensions—especially when more retirees live alone and look to the state for care rather than to their families.

Western nations have also experienced a decline in birth rates. Women have fewer children than they did in the mid-20th century, with the result that the populations of many European and Scandinavian nations are not reproducing themselves. These trends have produced major changes in the age composition of European populations with ever-fewer workers paying for ever-more retirees. (American birth rates are above replacement level and immigration is high, resulting in a growing population.) When commentators talk of a demographic time bomb affecting pensions, entitlements, and healthcare, it is these trends they have in mind.

Migration and cultural change

Social provision meets less resistance in societies exhibiting high levels of social solidarity and fellow feeling. Small, homogeneous nations—such as Norway, Sweden, and Denmark—tend to have more generous, more inclusive welfare states than do large, heterogeneous countries such as the USA. It matters, therefore, that in recent decades western nations have experienced large waves of immigration and have become more ethnically and religiously diverse. In the early 1990s more than 10 million EU residents were nationals of non-European states, and a further 5 million were EU nationals who had moved between member nations. Even Sweden is becoming more diverse: 12 per cent of Swedes are now foreign born and about a quarter of those under 18 are immigrants or the children of immigrants. As a result, the solidarities upon which welfare states rely are becoming more difficult to sustain. Consider, for example, how the claims that EU migrants make on national welfare states have become a source of political tensions in the UK, where stories about East European migrant workers and 'benefit tourists' have scandalized the public and fuelled anti-EU sentiment.

In other respects too, welfare states now operate in cultural settings that differ from those of the 1940s and 1950s. Individuals born in the post-war years came to have values, tastes, and expectations that bore little resemblance to those of their parents who lived through the Great Depression and World War II. Decades of job security and rising wages produced relatively affluent middle classes for whom collectivist protections seemed less necessary and who expected higher quality services and benefits. Where welfare states failed to keep up, affluent workers turned to the private sector; becoming less supportive of welfare institutions and less willing to pay taxes to fund them. (As US House Speaker Tip O'Neill complained: 'We in the Democratic Party raised millions out of poverty, and made them so comfortable they could become Republicans!') Only where welfare states took care to sustain high-level benefits and quality services did they retain the crucial support of their middle classes.

American industrialist Henry Ford wrote in 1922 that 'Any customer can have a car painted any color he wants so long as it is black.' Over time, the basic, standardized tastes that Fordism presupposed were replaced by the more varied tastes and lifestyles of a more differentiated society of individuals. Where depression, total war, and post-war austerity had taught 'we're all in this together', decades of peace and prosperity saw the re-emergence of social fragmentation and a less collectivist ethos. This intensified individualism was fostered by consumer capitalism: by its market differentiation, its advertising, and its stress on lifestyle choice and expressive individuality. But it was also an effect of welfare states, which reduced the dependence of individuals on family and neighbours and provided them with autonomy and choices they would not otherwise have. Paradoxical as it seems, the welfare state has been a powerful vehicle for the spread of individualism.

WS 1.0 was designed to meet the needs of 'the industrial worker', 'the common man', and 'the average family'. It operated at the level of national aggregates—the national economy, macro-economic processes, the population as a whole—thereby deriving the benefits of scale, of large-scale risk pooling, and of uniform administration. And it addressed itself to 'employees', 'families', 'the unemployed', and 'old age pensioners' on the assumption that these were relatively homogeneous groups that had similar needs and preferences. The post-war welfare state was premised on the possibility of aggregation, of common experience, and of collective address.

The increasing importance of individualism and social differentiation—and the powerful processes of disaggregation that they bring about—has brought these assumptions into question. So too has the fragmentation of social classes; the decline of trade unions and political parties; and the destabilizing of families and communities. The category of 'the unemployed', for example, no longer refers to a relatively homogeneous group of out-of-work male breadwinners. It now includes the underemployed; part-time or temporary workers; people who stay in school or retire early because they cannot find work; people who are deemed disabled but who are really unemployed; the long-term unemployed; and those who are temporarily out of work as they move between jobs. One-size-fits-all benefits become increasingly inappropriate, as do the associated techniques of comprehensive risk pooling and mutualization. Social programmes have had to become more individuated and better adapted to the situations and biographies of specific individuals. Long-term processes of collectivization are being countered by new processes of individualization—and welfare states are caught in the crosscurrent.

New social risks

Ageing populations raise the cost of pensions, healthcare, and social services. More joblessness increases demand for benefits and reduces revenues. Family break-up and lone parenting increase the number of women and children in poverty while reducing the private welfare provided by family networks. And so on. But serious as these cost pressures are, a more fundamental difficulty is that today's precarious labour markets and unstable families generate a set of new social risks (NSRs) that unreconstructed welfare states fail to address.

Welfare states are elaborate and effective risk-management machines but today they encounter risks for which they were not originally designed. WS 1.0 addressed labour market risks by promoting full employment and providing social insurance, with social assistance for those who fell through the cracks. New phenomena such as long-term joblessness, precarious employment, and destabilized families reveal the limits of social insurance and change social assistance from a marginal form of welfare to an increasingly central one. At the same time, older social risks such as mass unemployment have reappeared in the wake of the global financial crisis, testing the coping capacities of standard social insurance. The challenge that welfare states now face is to develop policies that address the new social risks while renewing their capacity to manage the old ones; a challenge that the neoliberal reforms of WS 2.0 did little to meet.

So what exactly are these new social risks? Whom do they affect? And what are the new policies designed to deal with them? One set of NSRs stems from the dualized, precarious character of contemporary labour markets. Long-term unemployment and social exclusion; part-time or temporary work that brings insufficient security; career interruptions that reduce pension entitlements; having one's skills become obsolete in mid-career; and being 'working poor' (i.e. full-time employed while earning poverty-level wages) are all examples. A second set—resulting from changes in family forms, gender relations, demography, and migration—includes being a single parent; being a divorced spouse; a child living in poverty; a dual-earner couple or lone working mother experiencing difficulties obtaining childcare or balancing work and family life; the very elderly in need of intensive support; and immigrants experiencing social and cultural exclusion.

The people most affected by NSRs are poorly organized, do not belong to trade unions, have little political power, and are ill-served by both WS 1.0 and WS 2.0. And the hazards to which these groups are exposed include marginalization and social exclusion as well as impoverishment. Welfare states are increasingly facing large groups who are disconnected from mainstream social life as well as from economic opportunities.

Towards WS 3.0

The more radical reform proposals prompted by the NSRs—a global tax on capital; a guaranteed minimum income; stakeholder schemes that provide a capital endowment to every child; the creation of a European welfare state; the re-establishment of Bretton Woods—have gained little traction in today's political climate, though they hold out new horizons of possibility and act as vital reminders of what might be achieved given the support of powerful social actors or the effective mobilization of popular reform movements. Instead, the themes that have come to dominate the mainstream policy agenda are *social investment* (making social policy a productive factor by enhancing human capital, improving productivity, and increasing labour market participation); *individuation* (adopting more varied, more customized interventions that better fit the needs of diverse groups and individuals); and *gender-sensitivity* (promoting policies that cater to the specific needs of women and children); together with the ongoing concern to ensure the future solvency of pensions and healthcare.

The leading form of social investment—now the official aim of welfare regimes everywhere—is known as *labour market activation*. Instead of a passive welfare state that pays for long-term unemployment and in effect funds social exclusion, activation policies aim to provide people with the support they need to move back into the labour market and to build 'social bridges' enabling non-standard jobs to lead to more sustainable careers. At the core of these policies is a concern to increase human capital, to enhance the skills and employability of individuals, and to remove obstacles that stand between them and employment. Instruments currently in use include: continuing education; training and retraining; skills development; work experience programmes; job search assistance; job creation schemes; and the provision of public sector employment. A further, related measure is the 'Earned Income Tax Credit' (EITC) which subsidizes low-paid employees in an effort to lift the working poor out of poverty. EITC has been adopted in the USA and the UK with some success but other nations have been reluctant to adopt it lest it subsidize unproductive employers (as Speenhamland did in the 19th century) and reduce workers' incentives to upgrade their skills.

Post-industrial security

As well as moving people into work, welfare states have had to adapt their arrangements to fit reconfigured labour markets that no longer resemble those of WS 1.0. Instead of making social insurance available only to workers in continuous full-time employment, the new aim is to make social security more flexible and extend it to people in non-standard contracts of employment. By offering insurance cover and employment protections to part-time and temporary workers (or to job-sharers) flexible labour markets can be rendered less precarious and insecure. And these 'flexicurity' arrangements make it more feasible to relax employment regulations and facilitate fixed term employment contracts, thereby encouraging job creation. The new guiding principles are flexibility and individuation: offering individuated assistance rather than uniform, one-size-fits-all provision.

Labour market and demographic changes have also put pension reform on government agendas everywhere. To adapt to today's varied and non-standard employment patterns, pension schemes will have to become more inclusive, enrolling part-time and temporary workers and covering individuals (overwhelmingly women) who provide unpaid care or take career breaks to care for children and relatives. At the same time, efforts are being made to improve the actuarial standing of existing schemes to deal with demographic projections and worsening dependency ratios. Healthcare and social care costs are similarly affected and are also under intense scrutiny.

Pension reform is highly political and all the major reform options encounter strong opposition. The retirement age could be set higher, which would require workers to contribute for longer and to draw benefits for fewer years. This option would produce immediate, large savings but all of its costs are imposed on older workers, most of whom want to retire as soon as it is economically feasible. (The statutory retirement age in much of Europe is currently 65 but the average real retirement age is 58 or 59.) An alternative would be to increase contribution levels across the board—which would hit low-paid workers—or to make higher-earning employees pay more: e.g. by removing the cap on earnings liable for contributions or making contributions more steeply progressive. Cutting pension benefits is a third option, but in many nations the elderly rely on pensions for their basic income. In the USA, for example, those in the bottom 40 per cent of the elderly population get 83 per cent of their income from social security.

Contemporary social policy is adapting to changing family forms by recognizing same-sex partners, providing support for single parents, and improving social services for the elderly. But the major thrust of current policy change is the development of more women-friendly approaches that enable more women to participate in the workforce (thereby adding to welfare state revenues and reducing dependency rates) and supporting working women's ability to raise children and have a satisfying family life (thereby upholding fertility rates and reproducing the workforce). Women-friendly policies include support for working mothers and those with care responsibilities; pension credits for child-rearing; paid parental leave; affordable childcare; and provision for work absence when children are ill. Social services for the elderly are also women-friendly since it is mostly women who would otherwise provide unpaid care. The expansion of social services for the poor, the young, the old, and the excluded are also possible ways of addressing NSRs.

NSR reform and welfare regimes

Programmes addressing NSRs have developed at different paces in different nations—despite the Lisbon Strategy on economic reform and social cohesion which encouraged EU member states to coordinate reform efforts. The Nordic nations already have highly developed policies for women and active labour market policies. Sweden has had an active labour market policy since the 1950s, offering retraining, assistance with job placement, and, as a last resort, public sector jobs. (More than 25 per cent of the Swedish workforce is employed in government or public sector jobs.) By contrast, Germany's welfare state, like that of other conservative regimes, continued until recently to bias its support towards male workers; to exhibit low labour force participation rates and low fertility; and to do little to address the risks associated with unemployment and family change. Liberal regimes have done more than the conservative regimes in this regard though some of their policies—most notably 'workfare'—have tended to be more disciplinary than protective. With respect to pension reform, the UK is raising the age of retirement from the long-standing thresholds of 65 (for men) and 60 (for women) up to 68 by the middle of 2030s, by which time the gender differential will be phased out. In the USA, the age at which full Social Security pension benefits are available is set to rise from 65 to 67, though partial benefits can be taken at age 62.

Some of this variation between regimes is an accident of timing. The shift to post-industrialism occurred earlier in the Nordic nations, at a time when welfare states were still expanding and could more easily adapt. Other nations found adaptation more difficult because NSRs emerged in a period when their welfare states were undergoing retrenchment. More generally though, the pattern of national response to the NSRs maps onto the familiar pattern of regime variation described in Chapter 5.

The politics of welfare reform

States exercise power but they also solve problems. And the effort to shape a third generation welfare state is an example of how states adapt to change and learn from prior experience. But even when technical policy solutions have been effectively developed, political difficulties stand in the way of change.

Long-established welfare programmes have created constituencies of support with powerfully vested interests and a settled expectation of retaining them. The result is that insiders entitled to benefits are pitted against outsiders who are not. In many nations today a majority of the electorate prefers to preserve the current welfare state rather than reform it to better serve outsiders and future generations. Compounding these difficulties is the absence of short-term electoral rewards for political parties that seek to make necessary but painful long-term adjustments; and the fact that some of these changes will need to be supra-national.

The post-war welfare state was created with the support of powerful social movements amidst a worldwide crisis of capitalism and democracy. Today, the crisis is a low-intensity one, with poorly organized groups experiencing the worst of it. The challenge for governments everywhere is to carry through future-oriented changes and create reformed welfare states that effectively address contemporary risks while simultaneously enhancing economic efficiency. Well-adapted, high functioning welfare states are essential for modern capitalist democracies but the political challenges of building them can hardly be underestimated. And the more fractious and dysfunctional our polities become, the more difficult it is to assemble the coalitions and compromises upon which successful social policy depends.

Chapter 9
The indispensable welfare state

I want to conclude my account of the welfare state by setting out an argument that encapsulates the historical and sociological ideas discussed in the book so far. I want to insist that the welfare state is not a policy option that we are free to adopt or reject at will. Nor is it a phase of post-war history that we are now leaving behind. The welfare state is, instead, a fundamental dimension of modern government, absolutely integral to the economic functioning and social health of capitalist societies. Welfare regimes can take a variety of different forms, and can be more or less effective, but a welfare state of some description is a vital part of any modern nation.

We can make this claim in its most concise form by stating that in contemporary western societies the welfare state is what the classical sociologist Emile Durkheim described as a 'normal social fact' (and by 'normal' Durkheim means functionally essential and integral to social health).

Durkheim sets out two criteria by means of which we can classify a social institution as normal or abnormal. A normal social fact is an institution or collective arrangement that (i) exists in all societies that have reached a comparable stage of development; and (ii) is bound up with, and integral to, the functioning of these societies.

It is an easy matter to show that the welfare state meets the first of these criteria. The welfare state exists, in some version or other, in every developed society that has an industrial or a post-industrial economy. And that continues to be true even after three decades of assaults on the welfare state by neoliberal policy reforms. In the USA and the UK, anti-welfare politics have transformed aid to the poor, reducing benefit levels, and tightening eligibility conditions. Anti-union legislation—along with structural changes in the labour market—has reduced workplace freedom, increased income inequality, and made working-class households more insecure. And the UK and US economies are nowadays governed less by Keynesian demand management and more by monetary controls and supply-side interventions. But all of these changes have had little impact on the welfare state's institutional core. Social Security and Medicare in the USA, and National Insurance and the NHS in the UK, have expanded over that time and continue to command massive popular and political support—a pattern of persistence in adversity that is replicated in all of the OECD nations over the same period. Today's welfare states have been transformed in important respects but, as shown in Chapter 7, their infrastructures remain firmly in place and they remain a vital dimension of modern government and of social and economic life.

The second test is more complicated. How can we show that the welfare state is essential to the functioning of developed capitalist societies? How can we demonstrate that it is, as Durkheim put it, 'bound up with the fundamental conditions of social life'?

Here we need to recall some of the harsher characteristics of capitalist economies and competitive markets—features that we often forget precisely because welfare states moderate and obscure their effects. Modern societies are *capitalist* societies. They are, to paraphrase the German sociologist Wolfgang Streeck, societies that have set up their economies in a capitalist manner and in so doing have entrusted the vital task of material provision (upon which all human life depends) to private economic actors—i.e. to capitalist firms whose actions are oriented towards the accumulation of capital on the basis of private calculations of utility.

Capitalism is, it should be said, a tremendously powerful system of production and exchange. No other economic system can compare in terms of sheer productivity, innovation, and dynamism. And capitalism's impact on technological progress and the accumulation of goods is unsurpassed in human history.

Open markets also have their virtues. They are remarkable arrangements for generating choice, communicating information, and promoting certain kinds of freedom and equality. And the worldwide expansion of trade and commerce has, if some historians are to be believed, contributed to the softening of manners, the expanded scope of solidarities, and the civilizing of nations. In all these respects, capitalist economies have been an enormous boon to human welfare.

But there is also a fundamental sense in which capitalism, as a system of economic action, is profoundly *anti-social*. Societies that allow economic life to be governed by the logic of private profit and market competition are societies at risk. They are prone to rapid undirected change; to socially damaging concentrations of wealth and inequality; to crises of accumulation; and to periodic economic collapse—sometimes on a worldwide scale. The chief characteristics of capitalist societies are not stability and equilibrium: these are the unfounded assumptions of economic theory, not facts about real world economies. The chief characteristics of capitalist societies are uncertainty, insecurity, inequality, and undirected change—all of which generate damaging consequences for our social and natural environments.

As Marx and Engels pointed out long ago, capitalism permanently revolutionizes the societies it inhabits. It generates what the economist Joseph Schumpeter called 'creative destruction' leaving a trail of disruption in its path. We see this all the time: in the collapse of the old industrial sector, the 1970s oil shocks, the 2008 housing bubble, the Eurozone crisis, the global financial crisis, all of which caused massive disruptions to people's lives. But even as it brings social disruption in its wake, profitable capitalist action requires a supportive social environment and an enabling material infrastructure. It needs socialized, educated, healthy workers—and the functioning families, communities, schools, and healthcare systems that produce them. It needs a dependable supply of raw materials and resources; a transportation infrastructure; a population of consumers; a stable political environment and much else besides (see Box 14).

Left to their own devices, competitive markets and private profit-seeking tend to destroy these essential social supports. Their tendency is to commodify, to consume, to expand, and to destroy all obstacles that stand in the way of accumulation. And these capitalist processes produce disastrous side-effects—as witness the threats currently affecting the climate, our natural resources, family life, and the physical and economic health of populations.

Box 14 Private enterprise and social provision

'There is nobody in this country who got rich on their own. Nobody. You built a factory out there—good for you. But I want to be clear. You moved your goods to market on roads the rest of us paid for. You hired workers the rest of us paid to educate. You were safe in your factory because of police forces and fire forces that the rest of us paid for. You didn't have to worry that marauding bands would come and seize everything at your factory—and hire someone to protect you against this—because of the work the rest of us did.'

US Senator Elizabeth Warren, 2011

Market capitalism is, to quote Streeck again, an inherently 'self-destructive social formation' which is protected from the dangers it creates by the operation of anti-market and market-moderating processes. The paradoxical—one might say *dialectical*—consequence is that 'capitalism depends vitally on the presence, essential but never guaranteed, of effective opposition to it'. To avoid self-destruction capitalism needs a set of countervailing forces. And welfare states are the embodiment of these forces established in a functional, institutional form.

Beveridge, Keynes, and their contemporaries recognized the uncertainty, instability, and anti-social effects generated by capitalist processes. They designed an apparatus that would manage these uncertainties, flatten out booms and busts, and establish a framework of collective economic security in which capitalist risk-taking might proceed. Since that time, the social regulation of markets, the social insuring of workers, and the public provision of social services and protections—in short, *the welfare state* in one or other of its variants—has become our established means of restraining the anti-social dynamics and the destructive externalities that are the essential concomitants of free-market capitalism.

The genius of the welfare state is its capacity to use the magic of averages and the collectivization of risks to render market capitalism habitable for humans and compatible with modern democracy. We have seen how the enfranchisement of working people, beginning in the early 20th century, meant that the power of private ownership came to be tempered by the power of governmental action and public law. And though the quality of government varies—and constant vigilance is needed if the effects of ineptitude, corruption, overreach, and special interests are to be minimized—the record of the last hundred years shows that welfare state government can succeed in civilizing and democratizing the stupendous power of capitalist enterprise.

Critics of these arrangements describe the welfare state as a hindrance to economic and social vitality. But the analysis presented in this book suggests the exact contrary: that welfare states are an essential means of *sustaining* that vitality.

Welfare state programmes are, for reasons I have indicated, inherently problematic and non-ideal. And today they are everywhere under stress and in need of adaptive reform. But they are also an essential counterweight to problem-prone capitalist economies that could not exist without them. Once we establish that historical and sociological truth, and put an end to the destructive dismissal of the welfare state project, we can more clear-sightedly turn to the task of improving welfare state institutions and adapting them to the social and economic challenges of our time.

References and further reading

For a comprehensive overview: Francis Castles, Stephen Leibfried, Jane Lewis, Herbert Obinger, and Christopher Pierson (eds.), *Oxford Handbook of the Welfare State* (Oxford University Press 2010). For a selection of classic and contemporary articles: Christopher Pierson, Francis Castles, and Ingela Naumann (eds.), *The Welfare State Reader*, 3rd edn. (Polity 2014).

Chapter 1: What is the welfare state?

On misunderstandings and myths: T. Marmor et al., *America's Misunderstood Welfare State: Persistent Myths, Enduring Realities* (Basic Books 1990); John Hills, *Good Times, Bad Times* (Policy Press 2015).

Sources of quotations in this chapter: William Beveridge, *Social Insurance and Allied Services* (HMSO 1942); Richard Titmuss, *Essays on 'the Welfare State'* (Allen & Unwin 1963); T. H. Marshall, 'Citizenship and Social Class', in *Sociology at the Crossroads* (Heineman 1963). UK government spending information: <http://www.ukpublicspending.co.uk/uk_budget_pie_chart>

On normative justifications for the welfare state: Robert Goodin, *Reasons for Welfare* (Princeton University Press 1988).

Chapter 2: Before the welfare state

Social provision in Roman antiquity: Paul Veyne, *Bread and Circuses: Historical Sociology and Political Pluralism* (Penguin 1992).

Pre-industrial provision: Paul Fideler, *Social Welfare in Pre-Industrial England* (Palgrave 2006); The 'protector state': Michael Walzer, *Spheres of Justice* (Basic Books 1984); Charity in Islam: Amy Singer, *Charity in Islamic Societies* (Cambridge University Press 2008).

Reciprocity and beneficence: Marcel Mauss, *The Gift: The Form and Reason for Exchange in Archaic Societies* (Norton 1990); Alvin Gouldner, 'The Importance of Something for Nothing', in *For Sociology* (Penguin 1975).

Welfare's religious roots: Sigrun Kahl, 'The Religious Roots of Modern Poverty Policy: Catholic, Lutheran, and Reformed Protestant Traditions Compared', *European Journal of Sociology* 46(1) (2005), 91–126.

The English Poor Laws: Lynn Lees, *Solidarities of Strangers: The English Poor Laws and the People, 1700–1948* (Cambridge University Press 2007). Public welfare in 19th-century America: William Novak, *The People's Welfare: Law and Regulation in Nineteenth Century America* (University of North Carolina Press 1996).

Moral economies: E. P. Thompson, 'The Moral Economy of the English Crowd in the 18th Century', in *Customs in Common* (New Press 1993); James C. Scott, *The Moral Economy of the Peasant: Subsistence and Rebellion in Southeast Asia* (Yale University Press 1976). Altruism and welfare states: Richard Titmuss, *The Gift Relationship: From Human Blood to Social Policy* (Penguin 1970); Michael Ignatieff, *The Needs of Strangers* (Picador 2001).

19th-century laissez-faire and social reactions to it: Karl Polanyi, *The Great Transformation: The Political and Economic Origins of Our Time* (Farrar & Rinehart 1944).

Chapter 3: Birth of the welfare state

For a selection of historic texts and key documents: Robert Goodin and Deborah Mitchell (eds.), *The Foundations of the Welfare State*, 3 vols. (Edward Elgar 2000).

General and comparative histories: Peter Flora and Arnold Heidenheimer (eds.), *The Development of Welfare States in Europe and America* (Transaction 2005); Peter Baldwin, *The Politics of Social Solidarity: Class Bases of the European Welfare State 1875–1975* (Cambridge University Press 1990); Abram De Swaan,

In Care of the State: Health Care, Education, and Welfare in Europe and the USA in the Modern Era (Oxford University Press 1988); Franz-Xavier Kaufmann, European Foundations of the Welfare State (Berghahn Book 2012).

'Modern social risks': William Beveridge, Insurance for All and Everything (The Daily News Ltd 1924).

The role of labour movements: Walter Korpi, The Democratic Class Struggle (Routledge 1983). On the politics of social democracy: Shari Berman, The Primacy of Politics (Cambridge University Press 2006). For an overview of theories explaining the rise of the welfare state: John Myles and Jill Quadagno, 'Political Theories of the Welfare State', Social Service Review (March 2002), 34–57.

19th-century state provision: David Roberts, Victorian Origins of the British Welfare State (Yale University Press 1960); Oliver MacDonagh, 'The Nineteenth-Century Revolution in Government: A Reappraisal', The Historical Journal 1(1) (1958), 52–67.

New Liberal and Progressive ideas: Stefan Collini, Liberalism and Sociology: Political Thought in England 1880–1914 (Cambridge University Press 1983); Dan Rodgers, Atlantic Crossings: Social Politics in a Progressive Age (Harvard University Press 1998). On scientific charity: Gareth Stedman Jones, Outcast London: A Study of the Relationship between Classes in Victorian Society (Verso 2013).

Development of the American welfare state: Theda Skocpol, Protecting Soldiers and Mothers: The Political Origins of Social Policy in the United States (Harvard University Press 1992); Michele Dauber, The Sympathetic State: Disaster Relief and the Origins of the American Welfare State (Chicago University Press 2013).

Development of the British welfare state: Asa Briggs, 'The Welfare State in Historical Perspective', European Journal of Sociology 2(2) (1961), 221–58; Nicholas Timmins, The Five Giants: A Biography of the Welfare State (Fontana 1996).

Chapter 4: The welfare state 1.0

The hidden welfare state: Christopher Howard, The Hidden Welfare State: Tax Expenditures and Social Policy in the United States (Princeton University Press 1997); Jacob Hacker, The Divided Welfare State: The Battle over Public and Private Social Benefits in the United States (Cambridge University Press 2002).

Social insurance: Jochen Clasen (ed.), *Social Insurance in Europe*
(Policy Press 1997); Daniel Shaviro, *Making Sense of Social
Security Reform* (Chicago University Press 2001). Social assis-
tance: Linda Gordon, *Pitied But Not Entitled: Single Mothers and
the History of Welfare* (Harvard University Press 1994); Michael B.
Katz, *In the Shadow of the Poorhouse: A Social History of the
Welfare in America* (Basic Books 1996). Social work and social
control: Jacques Donzelot, *The Policing of Families* (Hutcheson
1980). Economic management: Peter Hall, *Governing the
Economy: The Politics of State Intervention in Britain and France*
(Polity Press 1986); Jim Tomlinson, *Public Policy and the Economy
Since 1900* (Oxford University Press 1990); John L. Campbell,
J. Rogers Hollingsworth, and Leon N. Linberg (eds.), *Governance
of the American Economy* (Cambridge University Press 1991).

The economics of welfare states: Nicholas Barr, *The Welfare State as
Piggy Bank: Information, Risk and Uncertainty* (Oxford
University Press 2001).

Welfare states and capitalism: Wolfgang Streeck, 'Beneficial
Constraints', in J. Hollingsworth et al. (eds.), *Contemporary
Capitalism: The Embeddedness of Institutions* (Cambridge
University Press 1997); Peter Svenson, *Capitalists Against the
Markets: The Making of Welfare States in the United States and
Sweden* (Oxford University Press 2002).

Chapter 5: Varieties

Welfare state regimes compared: Francis Castles (ed.), *The Comparative
History of Public Policy* (Polity 1989); Gøsta Esping-Andersen, *The
Three Worlds of Welfare Capitalism* (Polity Press 1990); Emanuele
Ferragina and Martin Seeleib-Kaiser, 'Welfare Regimes Debate:
Past, Present, Future', *Policy and Politics* 39(4) (2011), 583–611.

Capitalist political economies compared: Peter Hall and David Soskice
(eds.), *Varieties of Capitalism: The Institutional Foundations of
Comparative Advantage* (Oxford University Press 2001).

Sweden's welfare state: Bo Rothstein, *The Social Democratic State: The
Swedish Model and the Bureaucratic Problem of Social Reforms*
(University of Pittsburg Press 1996); Hugh Heclo, *Modern Social
Politics in Britain and Sweden* (ECPR Press 2010); John
Pontusson, 'Once Again a Model: Nordic Social Democracy in a
Globalized World', in J. Cronin et al. (eds.), *What's Left of the Left?*
(Duke University Press 2009).

Germany's welfare state: Wolfgang Streeck, *Re-Forming Capitalism: Institutional Change in the German Political Economy* (Oxford University Press 2009); Franz-Xavier Kaufman, *Thinking About Social Policy: The German Tradition* (Springer 2014).

America's welfare state in transition: Steve Fraser and Gary Gerstle (eds.), *The Rise and Fall of the New Deal Order 1930–1980* (Princeton University Press 1989); Premilla Nadasen, Jennifer Mittelstadt, and Maris Chappell, *Welfare in the United States: A History with Documents 1935–1996* (Routledge 2009).

Britain's welfare state in transition: Margaret Jones and Rodney Lowe, *From Beveridge to Blair: The First Fifty Years of Britain's Welfare State* (Manchester University Press 2002); Howard Glennerster, *British Social Policy: 1945 to the Present,* 3rd edn. (Blackwell 2007).

Patterns of policy change: Peter Hall, 'Policy Paradigms, Social Learning, and the State', *Comparative Politics* (1993), 275–96; Kees van Kersbergen and Barbara Vis, *Comparative Welfare State Politics: Development, Opportunities and Reform* (Cambridge University Press 2014).

Varieties of healthcare: T. R. Reid, *The Healing of America: A Global Quest for Better, Cheaper and Fairer Health Care* (The Penguin Press 2009). Varieties of social work: Christopher Jewell, *Agents of the Welfare State: How Caseworkers Respond to Need in the United States, Germany and Sweden* (Palgrave 2007).

US–Europe contrasts: Jonas Pontusson, *Inequality and Properity: Social Europe versus Liberal America* (Cornell University Press 2005); Peter Baldwin, *The Narcissism of Minor Differences: How America and Europe are Alike* (Oxford University Press 2011); Bruce Western and Katherine Beckett, 'How Unregulated is the US Labor Market? The Penal System as a Labor Market Institution', *American Journal of Sociology* 104(4) (1999), 1030–60.

Chapter 6: Problems

Reactionary rhetoric and its uses: Albert Hirschman, *The Rhetoric of Reaction: Perversity, Jeopardy, Futility* (Harvard University Press 1991).

Ronald Reagan's 'welfare queen' story: Josh Levin, 'The Welfare Queen', *Slate* 19 December 2013.

Criticism from the right: John Goodman, Gerald Reed, and Peter Ferrara, *Why Not Abolish the Welfare State?* (National Center for

Policy Analysis 1994); Daniel Patrick Moynihan, 'How the Great Society Destroyed the American Family', *The Public Interest* 108 (1992) 53–64; George Gilder, *Wealth and Poverty* (Basic Books 1981).

Criticism from the left: Claus Offe, *Contradictions of the Welfare State* (MIT Press 1984); Linda Gordon, 'What Does Welfare Regulate?' *Social Research* 55(4) (1988), 609–30; Frances Fox Piven and Richard Cloward, *Regulating the Poor: The Functions of Public Welfare* (Vintage 1993).

Feminist critiques: Nancy Fraser, 'Women, Welfare and the Politics of Need Interpretation', *Hypatia* 2(1) (1987), 103–21; Nancy Fraser and Linda Gordon, 'A Genealogy of Dependency: Tracing a Keyword of the U.S. Welfare State', *Signs* 19(2) (1994), 309–36.

The politics of welfare: Martin Gilens, *Why Americans Hate Welfare: Race, Media and the Politics of Antipoverty Policy* (University of Chicago Press 1999); Christopher Jencks, *Rethinking Social Policy: Race, Poverty and the Underclass* (Harvard University Press 1992); Mary Bane and David Ellwood, *Welfare Realities: From Rhetoric to Reform* (Harvard University Press 1994); Karen Gustafson, *Cheating Welfare: Public Assistance and the Criminalization of Poverty* (New York University Press 2012); Andrew Gamble, *Will the Welfare State Survive?* (Polity 2016).

Welfare states and redistribution: Julian LeGrand, *The Strategy of Equality: Redistribution in the Social Services* (Routledge 1982); John Hills, *Inequality and the State* (Oxford University Press 2005).

Chapter 7: Neoliberalism and WS 2.0

Libertarian and free-market critiques: Friedrich von Hayek, *The Road to Serfdom* (University of Chicago Press 1944); Milton Friedman, *Capitalism and Freedom* (University of Chicago Press 1962).

Neoconservative critiques: Charles Murray, *Losing Ground: American Social Policy 1950–1980* (Basic Books 1984); Lawrence Mead, *Beyond Entitlement: The Social Obligations of Citizenship* (Free Press 1986); Margaret Thatcher, *The Downing Street Years* (Harper Collins 1993).

Responses from the left: Fred Block et al. (eds.), *The Mean Season: The Attack on the Welfare State* (Pantheon 1987); Michael B. Katz, *The Undeserving Poor: From the War on Poverty to the War on Welfare* (Pantheon Books 1989); Tony Judt, *Ill Fares the Land: A Treatise on Our Present Discomforts* (Allen Lane 2010).

Neoliberalism and its impacts: Andrew Gamble, *The Free Economy and the Strong State* (Palgrave 1994); Paul Pierson, *Dismantling the Welfare State: Reagan, Thatcher and the Politics of Retrenchment*, rev. edn. (Cambridge University Press 1994); David Harvey, *A Brief History of Neoliberalism* (Oxford University Press 1995); Daniel Yergin and Joseph Stanislaw, *The Commanding Heights: The Battle for the World Economy* (Basic Books 2002); Andrew Glyn, *Capitalism Unleashed: Finance, Globalization, and Welfare* (Oxford University Press 2006); Jamie Peck, *Constructions of Neoliberal Reason* (Oxford University Press 2010).

Welfare reform and workfare: R. Kent Weaver, *Ending Welfare As We Know It* (Brookings Institute Press 2000); Desmond King, *Actively Seeking Work: The Politics of Unemployment and Welfare in the United States and Great Britain* (University of Chicago Press 1995); Jamie Peck, *Workfare States* (The Guilford Press 2001). Kathryn Edin and Luke Shaefer, *$2 a Day: Living on Almost Nothing in America* (Houghton Mifflin Harcourt 2015).

Privatization: James Meek, *Private Island: Why Britain Now Belongs to Someone Else* (Verso 2014); Nicole Marwell, 'Privatizing the Welfare State: Nonprofit Community-Based Organizations as Political Actors', *American Sociological Review* (2004), 69; Colin Crouch, 'Privatised Keynesianism: An Unacknowledged Policy Regime', *The British Journal of Politics and International Relations* 11(3) (2009), 382–99.

The New Public Management: John Clarke and Janet Newman, *The Managerial State: Power, Politics and Ideology in the Remaking of Social Welfare* (SAGE 1997); Julian LeGrand, *The Other Invisible Hand: Delivering Public Services Through Choice and Competition* (Princeton University Press 2007).

The return of inequality: Jacob Hacker and Paul Pierson, *Winner Take All Politics: How Washington Made the Rich Richer and Turned its Back on the Middle Class* (Simon and Schuster 2011).

The resilience of welfare states: Paul Pierson,'Welfare State Reform Over the (Very) Long Term' <http://www.lse.ac.uk/publicEvents/events/2010/20101109t1730vOT.aspx>.

Chapter 8: Post-industrial transitions: towards WS 3.0

The Bretton Woods system: John G. Ruggie, 'International Regimes, Transactions, and Change: Embedded Liberalism in the Postwar Economic Order', *International Regimes* 36(2) (1982), 379–415.

Post-industrialism and globalization: Gøsta Esping-Andersen, *Social Foundations of Postindustrial Economies* (Oxford University Press 1999); Pierre Rosanvallon, *The New Social Question: Rethinking the Welfare State* (Princeton University Press 2000); Fritz Scharpf and Vivien Schmidt, *Welfare and Work in the Open Economy*, 2 vols. (Oxford University Press 2000); Gøsta Esping-Andersen (ed.), *Why We Need a New Welfare State* (Oxford University Press 2002); Stein Ringen, 'Introduction' to *The Possibility of Politics: A Study in the Political Economy of the Welfare State* (Transaction 2006).

Cultural change: Daniel Rodgers, *Age of Fracture* (Harvard University Press 2012).

New social risks: Peter Gooby, *New Risks, New Welfare: The Transformation of the European Welfare State* (Oxford University Press 2005); Giuliano Bonoli, 'Time Matters: Postindustrialization, New Social Risks, and Welfare State Adaptation', *Comparative Political Studies* 40(5) (2007), 495–520.

Radical reform proposals: Nancy Fraser, 'After the Family Wage: Gender Equality and the Welfare State', *Political Theory* 22(4) (1994), 591–618; Philippe van Parijs, *Real Freedom for All: What (If Anything) Can Justify Capitalism?* (Oxford University Press 1995); Bruce Ackerman and Anne Alstott, *The Stakeholder Society* (Yale University Press 1999); Anthony Atkinson, *Inequality: What Can Be Done?* (Harvard University Press 2014); Thomas Piketty, *Capital in the Twenty-first Century* (Harvard University Press 2014).

Reform proposals: Commission on Social Justice, *Social Justice: Strategies for National Renewal* (Vintage 1994); Nathalie Morel, Bruno Palier, and Joakim Palme (eds.), *Towards a Social Investment Welfare State? Ideas, Policies and Challenges* (The Policy Press 2012).

The new politics of welfare reform: Paul Pierson, 'The New Politics of the Welfare State', *World Politics* 48(2) (1996), 143–79; Giuliano Bonoli, 'The Politics of the New Social Policies: Providing Coverage against New Social Risks in Mature Welfare States,' *Policy and Politics* 33 (2005), 431–50.

Chapter 9: The indispensable welfare state

On normal social facts: Emile Durkheim, *The Rules of Sociological Method* (Orig. 1897; Palgrave 2013). The welfare state as a normal social fact: David Garland, 'The Welfare State: A Fundamental

Dimension of Modern Government', *European Journal of Sociology* 55(3) (2014), pp. 327–67.

Elizabeth Warren quotation: <http://www.dailykos.com/story/2011/09/20/1018700/-Warren-Tells-It-Like-it-Is-No-One-in-This-Country-Got-Rich-on-his-Own>.

On capitalism: Joyce Appleby, *The Relentless Revolution: A History of Capitalism* (Norton 2010); Joseph Schumpeter, *Capitalism, Socialism and Democracy* (Routledge 1942); Karl Marx and Friedrich Engels, *The Communist Manifesto* (Orig. 1848; Verso 2012); Wolfgang Streeck, 'How to Study Contemporary Capitalism', *European Journal of Sociology* 53 (2012), 1–28.

Index

A

activation policies 127–8
administration, problems 84–8
age 122–3
agencies 61
  problems with 86

B

Bane, Mary and David Ellwood 90
banks, deregulation 104–5
beneficence 16–18
benefits
  claimants increased by generous
    welfare 89–91
  difficulties with applying for
    86, 88
  entitlement 91
  fraud 84–6
benefits of a new welfare state
  57–8
Beveridge, William 5, 29, 40,
  46, 47
birth rates 123
Bismarck, Otto von 68, 69
Blair, Tony 2
Bretton Woods 116–17
bureaucracy 86–7
Bush, George W. 109

C

Callaghan, James 101
Canada 4
capitalism 10–11, 20–2, 42–3,
  135–7
  laissez-faire 13, 14
charity 17–18, 33–4
Charity Organization Society
  (COS) 33
church, charity 17
Churchill, Winston 35, 56
Clinton, Bill 108
communism 41
conservatism 68–71
coverage of social insurance 60
criticism of welfare states 10, 81,
  83, 88, 92–3, 105–7
Crouch, Colin 105
cultural change 124–5
cultural diversity 123–4

D

definitions of welfare state 7–9
de-industrialization 118–19
  see also industrialization
demographics 122–3
dependency on welfare services 89,
  90, 91–3

SOCIAL MEDIA
Very Short Introduction

Join our community
www.oup.com/vsi

- Join us online at the official Very Short Introductions **Facebook** page.
- Access the thoughts and musings of our authors with our online **blog**.
- Sign up for our monthly **e-newsletter** to receive information on all new titles publishing that month.
- Browse the full range of Very Short Introductions online.
- Read **extracts** from the Introductions for free.
- Visit our library of **Reading Guides**. These guides, written by our expert authors will help you to question again, why you think what you think.
- If you are a teacher or lecturer you can order inspection copies quickly and simply via our website.

INTERNATIONAL RELATIONS
A Very Short Introduction
Paul Wilkinson

Of undoubtable relevance today, in a post-9-11 world of growing political tension and unease, this *Very Short Introduction* covers the topics essential to an understanding of modern international relations. Paul Wilkinson explains the theories and the practice that underlies the subject, and investigates issues ranging from foreign policy, arms control, and terrorism, to the environment and world poverty. He examines the role of organizations such as the United Nations and the European Union, as well as the influence of ethnic and religious movements and terrorist groups which also play a role in shaping the way states and governments interact. This up-to-date book is required reading for those seeking a new perspective to help untangle and decipher international events.

ECONOMICS
A Very Short Introduction
Partha Dasgupta

Economics has the capacity to offer us deep insights into
some of the most formidable problems of life, and offer
solutions to them too. Combining a global approach with
examples from everyday life, Partha Dasgupta describes the
lives of two children who live very different lives in different
parts of the world: in the Mid-West USA and in Ethiopia. He
compares the obstacles facing them, and the processes that
shape their lives, their families, and their futures. He shows
how economics uncovers these processes, finds explanations
for them, and how it forms policies and solutions.

'An excellent introduction . . . presents mathematical and statistical
findings in straightforward prose.'

Financial Times

CAPITALISM
A Very Short Introduction
James Fulcher

The word 'capitalism' is one that is heard and used frequently, but what is capitalism really all about, and what does it mean? This *Very Short Introduction* James Fulcher addresses questions such as 'what is capital?' before discussing the history and development of capitalism through several detailed case studies, ranging from the *tulipomania* of 17th century Holland, the Great Depression of the 1930s. In this new edition he discusses the fundamental impact of the global financial crises of 2007–8 and what it has meant for capitalism worldwide.

www.oup.com/vsi

GLOBAL ECONOMICS
A Very Short Introduction
Robert C. Allen

The gap between the rich and the poor can be vast. In this *Very Short Introduction*, Robert C. Allen considers the main factors that contribute to this gap, looking at the interconnections between economic growth, culture, technology, and income distribution. He also explores the historical processes that have created the unequal world of today, and takes a global look at wealth worldwide.

www.oup.com/vsi

LIBERALISM
A Very Short Introduction
Michael Freeden

Liberalism is one of the most central and pervasive political theories and ideologies, yet it is subject to different interpretations as well as misappropriations. Its history carries a crucial heritage of civilized thinking, of political practice, and of philosophical-ethical creativity.

This *Very Short Introduction* unpacks the concept of liberalism and its various interpretations through three diverse approaches. Looking at its historical and theoretical development, analysing the liberal ideology, and understanding liberalism as a series of ethical and philosophical principles, this is a thorough exploration of the concept and practice of liberalism.

www.oup.com/vsi

SOCIAL WORK
A Very Short Introduction
Sally Holland and Jonathan Scourfield

Social workers spend their time trying to ease social suffering. They encounter the extreme casualties of social inequality: the victims of poverty, illness, addiction, and abuse; they work with abusers and offenders; and operate in the space between the State and the poor or marginalized. In this *Very Short Introduction* Sally Holland and Jonathan Scourfield explain what social work is and the range of cases it deals with. Looking at its history and main debates, as well as the theories and methods of social work, they include a range of case studies from around the world.